Also by the Author

<u>BOOKS</u>

History
Birth of a Republic
The Civil War
The Life and Death of Michael Collins
A History of Irish Forestry
The Book of Irish Saints

Mythology
An Tain, Cuchulain's Saga, The Imperishable Celtic Epic
Deirdre and Other Great Stories from Celtic Mythology
The First Book of Irish Myths and Legends
The Second Book of Irish Myths and Legends
Irish Myths and Legends
Celtic Myths and Legends
Aspects of Parallelism in Japanese and Irish Character
and Culture

Fiction
Bottles and Old Bones

Pseudonymous
Life Has No Price (Desmond O'Neill)
Red Diamonds (Desmond O'Neill)
The Butterfly Murder (Susan Galway)
Crucible (Donal O'Neill)
Of Gods and Men (Donal O'Neill)
Sons of Death (Donal O'Neill)

Children
Murphy and the Dinosaurs (E. C. Francis)

Poetry
Poems from the Irish

<u>PLAYS</u>
The Earth a Trinket
Public Enemy
The Face of Treason (in collaboration)
Various radio and TV plays

3

For my old and good friends

Maire Og MacSwiney Brugha,
who kindly provided the introduction to this book,
the late C. J. Haughey who shared much with me
and the late Brian Lenihan
with whom I worked for so many years.

CONTENTS

ACKNOWLEDGEMENTS

I owe thanks to a number of people. They include in particular Máire Óg, as I always knew her, who suggested the publisher; Cathal Brugha and Manus O'Riordan who helped enormously in dealing with the publishers; Charlie Haughey whose interest and advice were always encouraging; the publishers themselves, of course, Jack Lane and all his colleagues at Aubane, and my old and close friend Darach Connolly whose exacting corrections helped banish most if not all solecisms, those that remain being mine alone, and who, while correcting it, reduced himself *ins na trithíbh dubhtha*.

My deepest thanks to them all.

INTRODUCTION

I have known Eoin Neeson for almost as long as he's known himself, since soon after he became a pupil at Scoil Ite, the school founded and run for many years in Cork by my aunts Maire and Annie MacSwiney.

So when he asked me to contribute the Introduction to *Myths from Easter 1916* I was very glad to do it.

Eoin's family and mine were connected before that. Our respective fathers, Terence MacSwiney and Sean Neeson, became friends in Frongoch after the Rising of 1916 and my mother, Muriel (Murphy), had long been a close friend of his mother Geraldine (Sullivan), who became my mother's bridesmaid. Both were accomplished pianists and pupils of the distinguished Cork pianoforte teacher, Frau Tilly Fleischmann and they all moved in that extraordinary, potent dynamic, with its powerful flavour of Mittel Europa, that was, and for a long time afterwards remained, a characteristic of Cork cultural life.

When this mixed, as mix it did, with the even more potent national movement embracing cultural (through the Gaelic League, for example), Volunteer and political activities, the effects were very strong indeed.

My father, when Lord Mayor of Cork, was also Brigadier of the Cork City Volunteer brigade, of which Sean Neeson was brigade intelligence officer. Both were teachers and, in addition, all four of our parents were very involved in cultural activities, Eoin's at professional level.

For many years now Eoin's books and writings have contributed significantly to our knowledge and awareness of recent Irish history. His pioneer work on the tragic civil war, *The Civil War in Ireland*, did much to clarify what, up to the time it was first published, was a period that had remained cloaked. It also helped readers to understand the forces and impulses that brought that sad event to pass. Prior to its publication in 1966 there was an open gap in the record of our history between 1922 and about 1925.

His more recent book, *Birth of a Republic*, is a ground-breaking narrative of republicanism from 1798 to 1923, and has been hailed as the best on this subject and period. While his *Life and Death of Michael Collins*, described by Lt. Gen. M. J. Costello as "the definitive account", provided the first in-depth analysis of the ambush in which Collins was killed.

He chooses themes that have been either deliberately ignored and by-passed – such as the civil war – or are allowed to remain confused and unclear, such as the narrative of republicanism from 1798 to 1923, or that have been misrepresented and distorted as in the case of the Rising, the subject of this book.

These books comprise a detached, important, balanced and informed consideration of how and why the country developed and evolved as it did between the Act of Union and the end of the Civil War.

In *Myths from Easter 1916* he again focuses on important aspects of our formative recent history – perhaps I should say on important distortions of it - and restores clear perceptions of reality where mendacity and misinterpretation were introduced.

In examining some of the mythic falsehoods that have often come to replace the truth about the Rising and its aftermath he also, so far as I know for the first time, disposes of them for the misrepresentations they are.

The average reader, no less than students of the period, owe him a good deal.

It is shocking to me to find that otherwise intelligent and estimable people can disparage and cheapen the very well-spring of the state – namely the Rising - that gave, and gives, them so much. (It may not be widely appreciated here, but the 1916 Proclamation is known abroad as one of the great democratic statements of our times and is referred to in that context side-by-side with, for instance, the American Declaration of Independence). If I judge their dismissive comments correctly, they do so mindlessly and with a startling ignorance of history. Eoin Neeson lays before us the reality and then asks – and answers – the essential questions. As always this book is enlivened by both the questing detachment of the historian and the lively, memorable prose of the author.

Nor is that surprising since Eoin's authorship extends considerably beyond history, though some of it is related. He has written a number of fine historical novels and is an authority on Irish mythology with some six books on the subject to his credit, the most recent of which, *An Tain, The Cuchullain Saga*, is, he tells us, the first time that the great epic of which the Tain is part has been presented in its entirety in modern, narrative, English prose. How I wish it had been available when I was younger. Under pseudonyms he has written thrillers and is the last of the so-called "Cork School of Realism" group influenced by Daniel Corkery, of whom Frank O'Connor and Sean O'Faolain are best known.

9

His identification of the Rising as "the focus of all preceding republican activity and the pivot on which subsequent separatist activity turned" seems to me to be precise and correct. With regard to the fact that the Rising and its leaders are today frequently the target of shallow prejudice and uninformed comment, he goes on to ask the question: - in whose interests is it to diminish the Rising and its leaders?

Strangely it is an important question that appears to have been lost in the witless scramble of those who, as he points out, are like Goldsmith's witless ones who "fashion doctrines on the hour that know and have an instant answer for all things" and wallow in self-applause. That their permissiveness goes so far as to tolerate national identity out of existence doesn't seem to trouble them. Though why tolerance and national pride and dignity should be considered mutually exclusive defeats me. In *Myths from Easter 1916* Eoin Neeson seeks to unscramble that issue and to answer that question.

Tolerance – amounting to chaos - that allots equivalence – and more – to prejudice and bigotry is dangerous and foolish. We have a proud and honourable tradition that must not be wrongfully eaten away and sabotaged by foolish and meaningless attempts to appease the unappeasable and tolerate the intolerable.

Here Eoin deals trenchantly and precisely with the prejudice directed at the Rising and with related and, (for all their airing in the popular press and by ill- or un-informed "revisionists"), aberrant questions.

It is a book for which there has been a long-felt need.

Maire MacSwiney Brugha, 2007

MYTHS FROM EASTER 1916

Eoin Neeson

Preface

IT IS A CURIOUS THING THAT, for some reason difficult to pin down, in Ireland the subject of history sometimes seems to acquire the character of a creative "art form". Contradictorily, particularly when it tells us that it seeks only that greatest of all historical dissemblers, "Truth", as if it hung in the darkened skies of the past waiting only to be plucked; this can also be called "scientific" historiography. Searching for concrete realities in the capricious and multitudinous "Truths" of the past may be an entertaining pastime in its own way, but it does not bring us a cohesive or coherent picture of what that particular piece of the past was all about so far as those who lived in it were concerned.

This book proposes to consider three current distortions of important aspects of the formative period of recent history and examine them with a view to correcting the false impressions and misrepresentations they give rise to.

Between 1910 and 1922 several occurrences that might, at another time, have gone down unrelated byways of history, coalesced in the spirit of those disordered times and, like an assembling storm centre, brought focus, direction and purpose to the often disparate political and social movements then stirring – as indeed they had been doing in a less focal way ever since the imposition on the country of the discordant Union with Great Britain in 1801.

The combination of factors brought together by forces outside themselves in those years shaped and gave birth to the Ireland we know today; the first sovereign Irish state for hundreds of years. And yet, astonishingly, even at this remove of close to a century afterwards, some of the vital facts of that brief period – in particular between 1916 and 1921 - are subject to serious misconstructions so that the reality often acquires the elusive character of a wraith that vanishes when you reach for it.

With three key events in particular the absurd situation arises that it is the distortions that are, nowadays, most often taken to be reality, while the facts are equally frequently ridiculed as fabrications or special pleading.

The three events and the associated questions are these: -

1.   Are there substantial – or any – grounds for the allegation that the final (third) British Home Rule proposals would, had they come about, have brought the same results as were achieved by the 1916 Rising and the War of Independence? Or is this a nonsense?

2.   A commonly accepted version of the military purpose and objectives of the Rising of Easter, 1916, is often held to have been a hopeless "blood-sacrifice" conducted by romantics and poets. Is this false, or prejudiced? What is the reality? and,

3.   Why did civil war break out barely one month after the Collins/deValera Pact of May 1922 that promised both an averting of armed hostilities and constitutional progress was agreed?

The answer to the first question - what Home Rule would have achieved - is difficult and elusive because here there is neither substance nor fact to support a proposition originating solely in (political) wishful thinking, sometimes illuminated, if at all, with that most exact of sciences, hindsight. It is a Tartuffian mirage hovering over some insubstantial desert of might-have-been – but it has occluded the reality very considerably.

The second question relates to the military purpose and objectives of the Rising. Contrary to what one might expect, it is perhaps the easiest of the three to answer since here we

14

deal with straightforward matters of fact even if distortion and manipulation, like giant, leafy weeds, falsify and obscure reality and the overwhelming balance of probabilities.

Our purpose is to identify these errors and allow the facts to speak for themselves. Identification is not too difficult. In the main it results from "Black Propaganda", a technique often credible and successful, particularly when, as in this case, it is constructed and trumpeted on a basis of possibility, however tenuous. The remarkable thing is that time helps it to be accepted and the facts to be dismissed. It is, accordingly, very good propaganda and very bad history.

With the third question there is a different problem to which finding a well-defined answer is the more difficult because the question itself arises from a determined refusal by successive waves of "experts" to assess and examine with detachment, the attitudes, motives and compulsions that bore on the issue – and more particularly on the people – involved in the question at the time. It is as if – and it might be so – these failures to examine and analyse the facts arise from a concern that to do so might suggest answers different to the ones the "experts" already prefer.

Why that may still be the case is hard to say. But, for instance, an article by a distinguished professor of history on the early days of the fledgling State (published within the past ten years) reads, in part, more like propaganda of the period from one side in the Treaty debate rather than an assessment by an objective historian.

Whether this kind of thing is a species of lingering, misplaced or inherited loyalty or tradition is hard to tell. Given the authorship and the fact that the teaching and writing of much third level Irish history has long been firmly in the hands of uncritical supporters of one side of the Treaty issue, it may simply be an attempt to select facts so as to present history for political or professional reasons. It may even be a refusal to reconsider what has hitherto, uncritically and without analysis, been held to be correct. In any case it distorts the reality of what happened.

The three questions derive directly from the persistent throb of republicanism that, like some vagrant jungle tom-tom, rose and fell, waxed and waned throughout the 19th century[1].

The events of history do not, like rocks rising grim and melancholy from an empty sea, occur in isolation. To be understood it is necessary to consider them in the climate of the times in which they occurred - by no means always easy

For the historian it is a challenge of understanding and interpretation as much as one of analysis. He or she must not – or, anyway, should not - seek just to recover the time, events and thinking of the period in question, but should also listen for the tempo and measure of its melody.

Perhaps because of shortcomings in this respect and also perhaps because of a prevalence of opinion and a rush for publication of hurried theses, we are today all too often offered pre-digested notions of historical facts measured – if at all – by today's values rather than by those of the period in question, often in a type of indigestible "historiographical" jargon.

Since, one way or another, our three questions derive from republican activity a brief resume since the Act of Union in 1801 may help put them in context.

It has been alleged that the first taste of republicanism in Ireland was Cromwell's Commonwealth – a statement generally, one imagines, made with tongue-in-cheek. For practical purposes, we can ignore it so far as Irish republicanism is concerned.

Robert Emmet's aborted rising of 1803, Pallas-Athena-like, came fully grown and armed into being, descended from the major republican rising of 1798 five years earlier.

Like Emmet's the '98 Rising was animated by the principles and political philosophies inspired by and developed from the French and American revolutions. It is an

---

[1] For a comprehensive narrative of republicanism and its development between 1798 and 1923, see *Birth of a Republic* by the author.

often unacknowledged fact that Emmet's Rising, had the hand of malevolent accident not decisively intervened, was likely to have proved more effective and to have better achieved its aims than 1798.

Between 1803 and 1860 republican activity waxed and waned but never died. There were protests in arms, small and smaller, every ten or fifteen years until the great famine and pestilence stalked the country together with their gaunt companion, death. Between 1847 and 1850 they halved the population (mostly poor and Catholic), of nine million or so, leaving behind a legacy of desolation that continued well into the 20th century.

Nevertheless, even in the desperation which all but caused every stone in the road and every surviving weed in the ditches to cry out at the horror of what they daily witnessed, there was, after the famine, some social and constitutional amelioration for the Catholic majority, wherein much, but by no means all, republican activity originated.

The Fenian movement was begun by Irish immigrants in America in 1854. After the American Civil War it came east again with veterans of that conflict and had a deep and abiding influence on post-famine Irish republicanism. Nineteen years later, in 1873, a Fenian convention in Dublin adopted the name Irish Republican Brotherhood (IRB) and it was in that form that it was to have its greatest and most powerful influence on subsequent events in Ireland. That convention adopted a constitution. It also passed two important resolutions that, though frequently overlooked, were to become critically important in the course of Irish political and military progress in the early 20th century.

These were: Firstly, that the central committee of the IRB constituted itself, and acted as, the government of the Irish Republic until such time as the Irish people freely elected its own government; and, Secondly, that the Head Centre, or chairman, of the IRB would also be President of the Irish Republic until such time, etc.

17

Between then and the Rising of 1916 there was considerable social and political activity and progress. Three things in particular can be marked out. Two of them arose from the revitalised spirits of a people downtrodden and exhausted after the famine and waiting only for the call of leadership to ignite their accumulated, suppressed and resentful energy. These were, firstly, the land agitations of the latter half of the 19th century that ended, in what was perceived as being a great and remarkable victory for thousands of farm labourers and small-holders throughout the country, the (George) Wyndham Land Act of 1903 broke up and divided amongst them many of the great ranches and estates that had been destroying their lives and livelihoods. Secondly, an urban counterpart to this rural agitation exploded some years later (1910-1914) – the bitterly opposed fight for social justice through trade-unionism - led by James Larkin, one of the most outstanding social agitators of the period, and the socialist writer and thinker James Connolly (neither, incidentally, a native of the country).

These movements that sprang with energy and agility almost spontaneously into Ireland, bearing aloft the bold banners of socialist thinking, were, like Fenianism, also imported from abroad – this time from England and the Continent. They took hold of the fears, anxieties and imaginations of the Irish working and labouring classes living – if it can be called that – in atrocious conditions in rural mud cabins and what were described as "the worst slums in Europe" (and that was saying something). They provided the motivation and impetus to inspire powerful and active righteous domestic social clamour and agitation.

At much the same time the Irish Parliamentary Party, then the only significant political voice in the country, changed direction under Charles Stewart Parnell, and, from being a mere collective of (often disparate) Irish voices in the British parliament, united and focussed its endeavours and its separate national identity until it eventually held the balance of voting power in Westminster, a power it proceeded to exercise with effect and purpose so far as Ireland was concerned.

The most important result of this activity was its contribution to the decision by the British Liberal Prime Minister, William Ewart Gladstone, to introduce Home Rule for Ireland, the first such Bill being moved in 1886.

It is clear, although it is also often overlooked, that Parnell's horizons were far from being limited to Home Rule and that he was actively considering – how deeply is beyond recall – giving his support, and that of the Irish Party, to the Fenian separatist movement, which had also been strengthening not only its purpose, but its base and following within the country. A hint of this is clear from Parnell's speech in Cork in January 1885, when he said: "No man has a right to fix the boundary of the march of a nation –".

The scandal resulting from his relationship with Mrs. Kitty O'Shea and the resulting divorce proceedings brought a sudden and untimely end to his charismatic and progressive leadership. This was followed soon afterwards by his death and, following that, such division and disruption in the Irish Parliamentary Party that the momentum gathered under Parnell slowed to a standstill. In fact Parnell was succeeded by new and lesser leaders and by a new and lesser objective: commitment to Home Rule as an end in itself.

Consequently the separatists, under the hidden hand of the IRB, and the divided and unsettled Irish Parliamentary Party, now found themselves following different paths.

In England a greater game was also being played in the last decade of the 19th century. Tory Opposition and the Liberal government were locked in what became a life and death struggle for power over what was then still the most powerful empire in the world. To win it control of parliament was vital. True, the Liberals were still in power, but their hold was shaky, and twice had their Home Rule Bills been defeated by the House of Lords. The Tories, like the lords, also strongly opposed Home Rule for Ireland and, in a situation where the number of votes separating

19

themselves from the Liberals was modest, and with the balance largely in the hands of the Irish Parliamentary Party, they decided that the Unionist votes in Ireland would win the day if they could only be garnered. So they set about trying to do so. It was a decision that was to have extraordinary consequences for both countries.

The bait was opposition to Home Rule, which meant limited domestic rule in Dublin with an essentially Catholic oriented administration.

The Tory reaction was paralleled by successive dilutions of the Home Rule proposal by the Liberal Government, also seeking to appease Unionist opposition.

Several unrelated factors then began to accelerate progress of the Tory/Unionist collusion until, like some subterranean monster that had been uneasily asleep, it suddenly erupted onto the hitherto more or less tranquil political pathways of Ireland from where, in the name of Unionism and with an instantly created army (the Ulster Volunteer Force), and, as 1912 gave way to 1913, and in open defiance of any attempt to introduce Home Rule, the illegal and essentially treasonable UVF rattled the political structures of Britain to their very foundations.

The third Bill, from which springs our first myth, went on the Statute Book of Great Britain just before the outbreak of the 1914-1918 Great War with the intention that it would come into force in Ireland in September of that year. As war loomed it was speedily suspended, indefinitely, as well as being simultaneously further diluted with the inclusion of partition for Ireland plus refusal of fiscal autonomy and other restrictions, all abruptly written into the Bill.

For Irish separatists this and the war were clarion-calls, not least because the war was promoted as being "for the rights of small nations". No sooner was it declared than they set about planning a rising that took place two years later – a rising that was the end of every republican separatist movement that preceded it and the inspiration and foundation of almost everything that followed.

What did follow was a volcanic transformation in the public mind and attitude to their rights as a nation. To suggest that before 1916 the nationalist thrust was a unified, homogeneous movement representative of the wishes of the people at large, would be simplistic and wrong. It was nothing of the kind. But it is from that base that our second myth developed.

As is almost universally the case when, like some political fermenting agent, a positive nationalist group is suddenly introduced to an otherwise apathetic and overborne populace and successfully begins to agitate the public mind, there was much political confusion in Ireland when war was declared and the British empire became involved.

The argument that The Rising was not inevitable is sometimes put forward, supported by statements such as "It need never have happened because Home Rule was on the Statute Book", or "Small nations were going to be recognised sooner or later, anyway", or "The people didn't want it" and the like. Such arguments provide a useful academic stimulus, perhaps, but one that is not sustainable. It is worth considering the relevant facts in context. Leaving the IRB aside for the moment, there had not been an armed insurrection (if one excludes the Land War activities) in the name of the nation for forty-nine years, more than a generation. There was, however, a strong dormant undercurrent of separatist energy available.

The unionists were preparing for war. They had arms and an army – the UVF - and had the backing of the Kaiser.

Had Professor Eoin MacNeill, distinguished academic and figure-head chairman of the Irish Volunteers, not provided the convenience and opportunity for the formation of the Volunteers under the hidden hand of the IRB, it would, sooner rather than later, have happened anyway under that aegis. Such a force would also, sooner or later, have attracted the attention of John Redmond (or another leader of the IPP). If that happened, and Redmond followed the course he

21

actually did, a similar split, emphasising the increasing public face of separatism, would have taken place.

There is no reason to suppose that the Irish Citizen Army, which was outside the sphere of influence of the IRB, would have acted differently, or that Connolly would not have goaded any other group of volunteers in the same way that he did.

Even if the IRB had not acted as it did, or did not exist, Clan na Gael and John Devoy in America would undoubtedly have plotted for a Rising.

While a majority of the people did not support The Rising and were not in favour of one beforehand, a *raison d'être* of The Rising - as repeatedly stated by leader after leader - was to revive a sense of separate national identity in the people as a whole. Thus, to argue against The Rising on the grounds that it did not have the support of a majority of the people in advance is inapt.

The essential questions are:

I. Could what 1916 achieved have been achieved otherwise than by a rising?

2. If the Rising had not taken place in 1916, would there have been a rising at all?

The answer to these questions has to be, respectively: "No" and "Yes".

The administration in Dublin Castle seemed to be afflicted with a kind of political inertia, looking on itself as little more than a caretaker administration filling in until – after the war, of course – a Home Rule executive eventually took over. It virtually shut down its eyes and ears so far as any intelligence about nationalist activities was concerned.

The strange declaration (at Woodenbridge, Wicklow, October 25th 1914) by John Redmond, Parnell's eventual successor as leader of the Irish Parliamentary Party (IPP), of support for the British war effort to the extent of offering his Irish National Volunteers as cannon-fodder added to the confusion and indifference. These lasted, certainly with uneasy moments, until the Rising – of which, for instance,

22

there was ample warning, which intelligence was first ignored and then, classically, misinterpreted. The Rising took place and was followed by the executions by the British of many of the leaders.

The executions helped shock people into political arousal and an awareness of the reality of the oppression under which they lived. Two years later, at the 1918 general election, and with overwhelming voice, they proclaimed their allegiance to Sinn Fein, the political arm of Fenianism.

That led to the formation of the first native - genuinely representative, if outlawed - government of the people, Dail Eireann, and to the War of Independence from 1919 to 1921.

Thereafter came a truce, negotiations and an Agreement (the "Treaty") between British and Irish representatives. But with the Treaty came also a split in what had formerly been a unified Sinn Fein. The split divided the Sinn Fein cabinet of Dail Eireann. It divided Dail Eireann itself; it split the army – the Volunteers, who had adopted or had conferred on them the 1798 republican cognomen, IRA – and it split the electorate. It threatened internecine armed confrontation, at which point Michael Collins, leader designate and chairman of the Provisional Government set up to administer the Treaty provisions, approached Eamon deValera, former President of the Dail and political leader of those constitutionally opposing the Treaty, with a view to resolving these differences, averting armed hostilities and bringing into effective operation a Sinn Fein coalition government that would administer the Treaty provisions on a republican basis.

The result was the Collins/deValera Pact a consideration of which – or rather a consideration of why it failed - provides the basis for our third myth.

It is around these events that, like the spores of some mendacious fungus, these three major myths settled - and spread a layer of misinformation over historical reality.

We will seek to rediscover what, deliberately or otherwise, has in each case been for so long obscure.

Finally we will also speculate about what might have been the outcome of the civil war had Collins not been killed at Beal na mBlath on 22nd August, 1922. In doing so it is possible – even likely – that we will be accused of doing one of the things to which we object in our Trinity of Myths. But that would be wrong. There is plenty of circumstantial and direct evidence to indicate Collins's intentions. Accordingly the coda to our Three Myths is an informed conjecture as to what was most likely to have resulted had Collins not been killed when he was.

Eoin Neeson, 2007

THE FIRST MYTH

The Vexed Question of
Home Rule

THE FIRST MYTH

The Vexed Question of Home Rule

IN TRYING TO CLARIFY EVENTS OF HISTORY one of the most difficult tasks for the writer is to try to get a firm and non-judgemental hold on what happened and why as seen and experienced by the people of the times in question. In trying to do this it happens often enough that instead of clarification one gets sometimes very complicated and difficult to understand theories and analyses instead of fact.

Those who were involved in the making of what we, in our later period, call history were coloured by the climate of the times in which they lived. In the majority of cases they were caught up in events and moved with them. In very few did they set out to, as it were, *make* history, as the occasional theorist and analyst would lead us to believe.

The question of whether Home Rule could have yielded the same ultimate result as 1916 and the War of Independence has become something of an historical quiz. So perhaps the sensible way to consider it is to try to start at the beginning (not always as easy as it seems either), and briefly outline how it came about; what it was intended to achieve; why it aroused bitter antagonisms and why it failed, sinking beneath the surface of the political morass of 1914, to be dragged again to the political surface by those who now wish to bestow on it a substance it never possessed.

Our search for the life and death of the Home Rule *mélange* that affected much political activity in Ireland and England for thirty years or more (1886-1918), starts oddly enough with the corruptly introduced Act of Union (1801) that affected relations between both countries for more than a century.

As the 1700s turned to the 1800s imperialism was the accepted and aspirational way of life in most of the civilised world, where the principle of expanding and protecting it was taken for granted. That, by the way, was to include the burgeoning United States whose progress towards imperial status and policies was even then underway[2].

At the turn of the 18th century imperial despotism was the norm and liberal resistance to it was generally seen to be anti-social and anarchic. Nevertheless the pursuit of human and civil rights and dignity, and in some cases sovereignty, bolstered by the example of France and the standard-bearing United States, began to gather force against a system that sat like a gigantic octopus with tentacles reaching literally to its ends, upon an all but helpless world.

After the Act of Union development of the movement for national self-determination in Ireland, while slow at first, did include a social dimension which was also opposed to the norm the Act sought to establish.

Henry Grattan's Irish parliament, which the Act had dissolved and replaced, was in no sense representative in

---

[2] It is illustrative of the cyclic nature of major formative forces of history that, when most of the rest of the world has all but abandoned the imperial principle, the United States, now the dominant world 'imperialist' power, pursues it vigorously under a somewhat lopsided banner in the name of Democracy. This may, or may not, be a good thing, but it is visibly happening.

modern political terms, differing little in that from most other parliaments of the day. But, although composed of an elite - exclusively Protestant – electorate, it had been an Irish parliament whose interests, such as they were, were vested in the country.

When it was swept away and Irish interests became subordinate to those of Britain, and Irish citizens were, *de jure,* reduced to the status of second-class British subjects, a curious situation also shambled into Ireland in the shadow of that flawed Act.

Like some illegal immigrant of our own times it was secretive and immature. But, if you except Emmet's aborted rising, tied as it had been to the coat-tails of 1798, it matured and strengthened until it began to exert a real influence. It was the concert of modern, active politics, not alone embracing the rights we have mentioned – but also reinforcing the means of achieving them.

The Act of Union was structured along the lines of the British/Scottish precedent of almost a hundred years previously. It was not only flawed, it was constitutionally outdated when it was introduced eleven years after the French Revolution and two after the republican Rising of 1798. It was destined to be a failure from the outset, and part of the answer to our question lies in how that predestined failure eventually took place.

"It is probable that after 1798 no form of government other than a republic could have emerged by popular acclaim in Ireland"[3].

Throughout Europe and the Americas political power in the hands of elite minorities was being threatened by a growing belief in Democracy and expanded suffrage. In Ireland the landowning elite, who also often administered the Act locally, were under systematic constitutional challenge in

---

[3] This point is elaborated on in the author's *Birth of a Republic*, p. 36.

all sorts of ways and were never able to establish similar controls to those their Scottish counterparts had long since benefited from. From the outset most of the political edifice of Ireland tottered and wobbled under the Act, and never really settled.

The exception was amongst the Dissenter population of Ulster which under it had essentially achieved all they had sought when they, too, participated in – and in many cases provided the leadership for – the 1798 Rising.

Amongst other abuses the Act led to absentee landlordism, what amounted to a policy of near genocide, to the massive ravishing and destruction of most Irish industries – including the already profitable timber industry (vital to cask-making and shipbuilding) and which, in the hands of covetous "undertakers" systematically destroyed Irish forests to the point where Arthur Young, in similar terms to other writers, observed that near Mitchelstown in County Cork "there were a hundred thousand acres in which you might take a breathing gallop to find a stick large enough to beat a dog ..."[4], while Boate, in his *Natural History of Ireland*, writing in Cromwell's time anticipated his words: "The great woods which the maps do represent to us upon the mountains between Dundalk and Newry are quite vanished, there being nothing left ... except one bare tree at the very top of one of these mountains".

Act of Union

No sooner had the Act of Union come into being than it faced parallel and powerful challenges. The first was a constitutional one and it came from Daniel O'Connell's Catholic emancipation movement. The second was Robert Emmet's Rising. From the British point of view that was potentially far more serious than the Rising of 1798. But for a

---

[4] *Tour of Ireland*, 1780.

disastrous accident it would have played havoc with the new Union since the rebels planned to seize Dublin.

Dublin had been seen as an Irish capital, the social counterpart of London, the glittering second city of the empire. Landowners lived there and on their estates, which they managed, and maintained a viable rural economy. All that changed after the Union, with appalling consequences. Dublin was abandoned by society and left to decline, while landowners became more noted for absenteeism than for land management. It was simply a matter of time until, with the growing population in Britain and the seafaring demand for salt beef, the realisation that cattle were more profitable on the land than people hit home. When it did, through agents operating on their behalf, the ruinous policy of closure and eviction that, as in the 18th century, caused poverty, disease and many thousands of deaths, started.

So we have the interesting question; what if Home Rule had been introduced instead of the Act of Union? The circumstances that might have enabled Home Rule to work at the beginning and throughout the nineteenth-century seem to have existed, while those for Union did not. But, for Britain, with the example before it of, on the one hand, Scotland and on the other of the American colonies, and with an expanding empire in India and elsewhere, Home Rule was not an option – not even a consideration. Had that not been so and had Home Rule, in fact, been introduced instead of the Act of Union, it is possible – though unlikely – that we might not now be wrestling with the whys and wherefores of this question.

But, curiously enough, the rebelliousness – common to intellectuals and the ordinary people alike - that might have been contained by Home Rule, remained alive in spite of some political progress from mid century onwards. But that was the very period when armed rebellion and the idea of achieving independence also developed.

It should also be recognised that the differences between the Scottish Act of Union of 1707 and the Irish one of 1801 were considerable. The conditions and circumstances at the time of the Scots Act led to its eventual general acceptance; the conditions and circumstances surrounding the Irish one did not.

In Scotland rebellion had been brutally crushed, the Highlands denuded and Dissenters scattered (many, ironically, to northern Ireland). The lowlander and compliant lords - in those days before the idea of democratic, human or sovereign, rights had developed constitutional legitimacy in Europe - accepted Union with Britain as their new political dimension.

What was worse from the Scots (royalist) nationalist viewpoint was that those who survived the purges felt betrayed by their leadership in France, and were further dismayed by the consequences of 1789.

In Ireland, on the other hand, awareness of separateness and sovereignty had not been lost, the people had been crushed, stamped on and betrayed; but they survived.

From its introduction in 1801 the Union was never accepted by the people and had been consistently opposed by various, sometimes powerful, organised bodies. Some, like Daniel O'Connell's Catholic Emancipation movement and the Irish Land League were primarily social movements. Some, like Isaac Butt's political party that led to the Irish Parliamentary Party, were constitutional movements. Some had a military tradition originating with the Rebellion of 1798 and stretching from it through Robert Emmet's aborted rising of 1803, the Young Irelanders and the Fenians in mid-century to the IRB that came to exercise such influence between 1870 and 1923.

Throughout the 19th century the question of national sovereign independence and the means of achieving it gained ground through these forces. So, while a case might be made for having introduced a system of Home Rule at the beginning of the 19th century, two powerful, opposing factors remain. The first is that even with Home Rule there would have been no guarantee that the republican demand for sovereignty would have been in any way diminished. The second is that by early in the 20th century political, economic and strategic circumstances had so altered that the idea of Home Rule, especially in its "diluted" forms as the most effective policy for Ireland was no longer valid anyway.

As early as the 1880's the Land League had become increasingly politicised; Parnell began to lean strongly towards sovereignty, and the physical force republican movement strengthened its traditions deriving from 1775, 1789 and 1798.

So why was Home Rule bound to fail? The answer surely lies in the effects of the great 19th century industrial revolution that changed perceptions – especially economic and social perceptions – everywhere.

Thanks to it and to political – sometimes revolutionary –activity there was an awareness of growing progress in social, human and electoral rights, all denied in Ireland where the great famine and trivial armed rebellions (usually republican inspired), were the most notable events of lasting importance. While industrial revolution and civil liberties raised standards elsewhere, a great majority of the Irish people were starving and living in utter poverty and degradation. Moreover it was a situation being exploited by Britain for her own economic benefit.

But Belfast was the exception to this general picture – a divergence that was to become increasingly significant. There Britain established shipyards and ancillary industries, bringing employment and basic prosperity to the region. But why not, for instance, have established these undertakings in Cork with its magnificent, developed, natural harbour ?

To answer that we must look at the demographic and political factors likely to have influenced the decisions.

Vital was the availability of a reliable, malleable, mainly planter and now (since the Act of Union gave them virtually all they had been seeking when they took up arms as republicans in 1798) loyal (Protestant) workforce which could be depended upon to uphold that loyalty on a sectarian basis in the face of extreme odds. In addition was Belfast's proximity to Britain and the Clyde.

Cork, with its great harbour, was fine – excellent as a naval base. But as an industrial base – that was an altogether different matter. Leaving aside the question of proximity to Britain, just how loyal and dependable might a workforce be that was drawn from an essentially rural, disaffected and almost entirely religiously primitive (Catholic) population? No contest. For these, and other, reasons such limited industrial development as took place in the country did so in the north entirely to the benefit of Britain.

It was partly on the results of such calculations that, in the early years of the 20th century, came powerful opposition to Home Rule.

Home Rule was meant to be subordinate to Westminster in all but some local affairs. It was to be a glorified form of restricted authority, specifically excluding such essential matters as control over customs and excise, fiscal affairs in general, foreign policy, land control, defence and other principal elements of governance. What, then, was it and how, why and when was it proposed?

In the last quarter of the century and coinciding with the accretion of influence to the IPP in the Westminster parliament when it held a critical balance of power, the physical force and socio/political movements began to coalesce significantly in Ireland.

In this restless climate and in order to achieve a compromise solution that it was hoped could satisfy the aspirations of the Irish and simultaneously retain British control of the country, the formula of Home Rule was concocted by Gladstone in 1886. In Westminster it promptly came to be seen not only as the most – indeed the only - politically acceptable and achievable concession that might be made to Ireland, but also as being extremely generous and enlightened. But only by the Liberal Party.

Home Rule was envisaged as being capable of satisfying the restless Irish, of protecting British interests and of attracting international commendation rather than the opprobrium that portrayal of the simian stage-Irish abroad had brought. For the IPP under Parnell things looked rather different. For them it was – at that time anyway - a sort of forerunner of Michael Collins's "stepping-stone" formula.

So, limited though the Home Rule proposal was, it in fact derived from the increasing influence and authority of the "three legs of Fenianism", the IPP, the Land League (now a powerful movement of great political potential), and the separatists, mainly IRB – as well as from the British Liberal Party. But it was vigorously and indignantly opposed by the Tory Party and the House of Lords.

That Liberal Party promotion of Home Rule was prompted as much by concern over the "three legs of Fenianism" proposing to march towards some unimaginable, disordered and probably - perish the thought - republican polity, as much as it may have been by concern for any prescriptive equity for Ireland, can hardly be doubted.

While Gladstone's initial attempts at Home Rule were defeated in the House of Lords, the third Bill, introduced by a successor Herbert Henry Asquith, was passed, but only after an Act of Parliament enabled a sufficient number of commoners to be ennobled to ensure its passage through the House of Lords – an ironic replay in reverse of the vote that carried the Act of Union through Grattan's Irish Parliament in 1800.

In Ireland cross-fertilisation between the Land League, the IRB and the IPP was not unusual. Under Parnell the IPP flirted with both the popular and influential Land League and the more secretive but no less influential IRB, as Parnell's mighty phrase "No man has a right to fix the boundary of the March of a Nation", suggests.

In the space of eighty turbulent and woefully traumatic years under the Union the people had acquired political voice and muscle. Prompted by example from other parts of the civilised world, a restless populace armed itself with weapons and with principles of self-determination. In

Ireland, where a labourer's wage was now only 2/3 that of his counterparts in Wales and Scotland and less than _ of those in England; where native industry and produce were depressed or prohibited to the benefit of England; where the population had been more than halved in the space of a few years and whose tradition of independence stretched more or less unbroken back into the dawn of European history, the voices of a people denied their sovereignty were again heard demanding political, civil and social justice.

As this outcry swelled means of achieving the goal also strengthened.

By and large (though by no means entirely or exclusively) the Catholic middle classes – well-to-do merchants, strong farmers, the emergent so-called "prof. classes" – conformed to the constitutional line. In general this meant support for the IPP.

But the bulk of the mainly disfranchised peasantry and working class turned increasingly to agitation and sporadic violence as their method of opposition to repression.

The secretive IRB, in some ways the most pragmatic of these three elements and which had already declared its Council to be the interim Republican government of Ireland, became the focal point of separatist thinking and activity.

The last quarter of the 19th century was a restless time of poverty, war and social unrest in Europe. Outright war excepted, this was nowhere the case more than in Ireland. Agricultural wages, as indicated above, were dismally low; of industrial wage there was virtually none except in the northeast. Land and house evictions were common, starvation was rife – a second famine barely averted – and disease was rampant. The slums of Dublin were notorious. Yet, through it all, fuelled by the "three legs of Fenianism", the principle of national purpose and objective was invigorated.

From the British perspective, of course, matters looked very different. There Irish unity of purpose, increasingly developing from mid-century onwards, was uneasily perceived as a sinister and formless – even republican – shadow stalking eastwards against the shining empire, to threaten British interests.

Since the Union Tory attitudes – and sometimes their methods – towards Ireland had ranged from contempt and coercion to what is today called ethnic cleansing (though that did not inhibit the IPP from voting with the Tories when they perceived a political advantage in so doing.)

Paradoxically, into this political quagmire fell the bitter divisions, discord and friction that followed Parnell's death which, temporarily, unexpectedly and powerfully endowed Home Rule with a substance it did not (and never would) in reality possess. The result was that things then changed. For no apparent reason, other than Parnell's absence, Home Rule took root. For many it may well have been seen as the least impossible objective, and, therefore, as the limit of ambition. Instead of remaining the rewarding, but boundless, milestone the astute Parnell had identified it became for his successors an objective terminus, a final trophy, an end in itself, to which they became committed.

Opposition to Home Rule

Insignificant though the Home Rule Bill was in terms of sovereignty for Ireland it aroused enduring Unionist passions. The idea, let alone its introduction as a Bill, ignited a furnace that roared into a devouring blaze which eventually consumed the British Liberal Party and, even until today, much of life of north-eastern Ireland[5].

---

[5] 'From that moment the excitement in Belfast did not subside. Eventually dangerous riots, increasing in fury until they almost amounted to warfare, occurred in the streets between the factions of Orange and Green. The police and combatants freely used firearms. Houses were sacked and men and women killed. The disturbances were savage, repeated and prolonged ...' Winston Churchill, *Life of Lord Randolph Churchill.*

Andrew Boyd, the contemporary northern historian, puts it bluntly:-

"a wave of terror, arson and murder swept through Belfast in the summer of 1886 ...".[6]

Anti-Catholicism was violently stirred up, not only in the north east of Ireland where it had smouldered for over two hundred years, but throughout Britain as well.

In the seven years between the first and second Home Rule Bills the British (Tory) Conservative Party manipulated Ulster Protestant loyalism to become the primary political weapon to (a) oppose Home Rule and (b) – the real purpose - to destroy the Liberal Party.

Accordingly when the third Home Rule Bill (1912) was introduced by Asquith it was passed and placed on the Statute Book in the sorry and transforming autumn of 1914 to the accompaniment of astonishing and unanticipated acts of treason and revolt – not from the Irish Nationalists – but by elements of the British Army itself and northern Unionists.

It also became a rare - if not the only – Bill ever to have been enshrined in the Statute Book of Great Britain that did not become empowered as an Act.

For this there were several reasons, not least the impact of war upon Britain and its Parliament, that – somewhat shakily, it is true – administered the convoluted affairs of a far flung empire, (no more troublesome part of which was that closest to home and directly affected by the Bill).

In spite of a history of sectarian violence in Ulster its sudden Tory-inspired, extreme and violent opposition to Home Rule seemed to leap dramatically from nowhere, even to the very banks of the Thames itself. The Unionist perception was that the Union that conferred on them the status (albeit second-class) of British citizenship and, more significantly, protected their Protestantism, was being undermined and threatened by Home Rule. Worse the

---

[6] In his book about the Belfast pogroms, *Holy War in Belfast*, Belfast 1969.

38

inevitable consequence of Home Rule for Ireland would be that they, the Unionists, would be governed by a largely Catholic administration in Dublin. Never!

Stirred to sudden, mindless and fanatical frenzy by the intriguing Tory Party, evidently totally unaware of the malignant power it was unleashing, the Unionists went so far, in 1913, as to appeal to the German Kaiser, a Protestant monarch, to come to their assistance. At the same time they set up a provisional government for Northern Ireland (area unspecified) and created an armed force (the Ulster Volunteer Force) pledged to resist Home Rule even to the point of rebellion against Britain (with or without help from the Kaiser).

At this point and in the light of Unionist rather than Nationalist action it is appropriate to identify both the basic flaw in Home Rule and the argument that it would have brought everything achieved by the Rising of 1916 and the War of Independence etc., - an argument which appears to be partly based on the assumption that it was Britain's right and within its power to dispense, or to withhold, sovereign status for Ireland.

Into the strange and trouble-filled scene outlined above – one, if not of promise, at least of possibility – now strode two grim figures, one more dour than the other. They were accompanied by a strange, circus-like, retinue infused, it seems, with a bigoted and passionate intent to prevent a resolution under Home Rule. With single-minded and hostile intent this caucus at once set about the business of endangering a peaceful resolution of any kind.

The two gaunt leaders were Sir Edward Carson, whose espousal of the Unionist/Protestant cause in the north of Ireland (though he was a Dubliner) was of the nature of a supernatural inspiration, and Bonar Law, the Canadian-born leader of the Tory Party, of Irish descent, whose inherited commitment to northern Unionism matched Carson's.

One curious follower of these men was an uncertain and dangerous Major Crawford, from whose statement that:- "If we are put out of the Union I would infinitely prefer to change my allegiance to the Emperor of Germany" – may be gauged some measure of the intensity of feeling and prejudice of the time.

Reinforcing this threat of unilateral action, and after considerable posturing and steaming about the North Sea and parts of the North Atlantic in a steamer leased with party funds, the same Major Crawford finally brought his ship, on 24th April, 1914, loaded with 30,000 rifles and munitions for the UVF, to Larne in County Antrim from, of course, Germany.

It is important to bear in mind that at the time Ireland, though occupied, was not a partitioned country. Partition did not exist, nor was it contemplated by the bulk of the Irish people. Ireland meant the entire island and everyone in it. Such writ as there was ran more or less equally – at least in theory - in Cork and Derry; in Coleraine and Clonakilty. Questions of political difference and allegiance were confined to a statutory context – at least until Unionists formed their (subversive) Provisional Government of Northern Ireland and sought help from the Kaiser to oppose Home Rule.

Compounding the muddle was the fact that the political dynamics underlying the Unionist/Home Rule face-off in Ireland had less to do with that country than with the struggle for political power in England then convulsing the Liberal and Tory parties.

The long and the short of it was that in their titanic domestic upheaval the Torys had decided – in the words of Randolph Churchill – to "play the Orange card" and, in so doing they hammered a stake through the coffin and heart of an already ailing Home Rule, so, in fact, quickening the pace of Irish self-determinism between 1913 and 1916.

In Dublin the treasonable moves by the northern Unionists were noted with considerable interest, particularly by the IRB. Following the establishment and arming of the UVF they established a similar (though for lack of funds, essentially unarmed) force, the Irish Volunteers. It remained largely unarmed until, in August 1914, some 1,500 rifles (also from Germany) were run into Dublin Bay and Wicklow in their yachts by Erskine Childers and Conor O Brien, respectively (not to be confused with Conor Cruise O'Brien)[7].

These activities of the Unionists produced another prospect, one initially unforeseen by the Tory Party inciting them. It was the threat that civil war in Ireland might result from their activities, which began to look quite likely as 1914 advanced.

That prospect had, of course, nothing whatever to do with the subsequent post-Treaty civil war and should not be related to it. But with prejudice and mounting passion, the threat did begin – and quite rapidly - to gather and to assume the lineaments of – what? An extraordinary, constitutional but also warlike, Unionist paradox that, instead of responding to the loyalties to Britain it claimed to hold dear, threatened instead to violently challenge them - on the battlefield if necessary and, if you please, with alien - in this case German - assistance.

And why did this extraordinary situation come about? Because the British Conservative (Tory) Party who deliberately stirred the restless and anarchic monster of Unionist prejudice, and then sought to manipulate it for their own purposes, grossly underestimated the forces they unchained.

They saw in the Ulster Unionist vote, strengthened by new leaders come grimly striding to purposefully dominate

---

[7] This development, while bearing on the Home Rule question, properly belongs to events leading to the Rising of 1916 and, while it might be both instructive and entertaining to trace them in the context of the increasingly impotent and collapsing Home Rule, that is not our purpose here. It is dealt with more completely and in its proper place in Part Two. Readers wishing to pursue a detailed account of this afflicted undertaking from start to finish are referred to the author's – *Birth of A Republic*, pps. 60-184.

the Unionist Party of northern Ireland, a means of toppling the Liberal government. What the Conservative leaders did not see until the danger was upon them, was that the prodigious creature they had unleashed was already almost beyond their control. Basically the loyalty of Unionism was to itself and its aims, rather than to the Tory party, or indeed to Britain.

Initially what it boiled down to was that these strange allies were united in their opposition to Home Rule. For Unionists that soon became a means to another end. Having been stirred to white heat by their own and Conservative demagogues, the question was: Where would the British Government stand in the event of civil war? Unionists flatly rejected any idea of Home Rule in the north of Ireland. As the differences between the Liberals and the Unionists became more heated during 1913, the prospect of civil war between the concentration of Unionists in northern Ireland and the largely nationalist remainder of the country began to seem more and more unavoidable. But then, in an attempt to offset the threat, the government started to modify its own Home Rule proposals even further.

After that events moved with considerable rapidity. The previous August (1912) Winston Churchill had written a letter to an astounded and suddenly helpless John Redmond in which he first introduced, rather as if it were an apparently harmless rodent easing through an aperture, the possibility of partition in Ireland. He didn't express it in such terms then; but, to the appalled Redmond, the meaning was clear when he read: "... the Tory Party ...see in the resistance of Ulster (to Home Rule) an extra-Paramilitary force which they would not hesitate to use to the full ... I think that something should be done to afford the characteristically Protestant and Orange counties a moratorium of several years before acceding to the Irish Parliament. I think the time approaches when such an offer should be made; and it would come much better from the Irish leaders than from the Government…"[8].

Carson also banged this drum when, a month earlier, he raised Home Rule in parliament and insisted that Ulster Unionists would not have it, managing at the same time to insinuate the principle of exclusion for Ulster from an Irish parliament. By September it was virtually a question of either/or; either the Unionists got their way on the question of Home Rule, or there would be civil war. By October parliament seemed to accept this when Bonar Law stated that he believed the nation was drifting towards the tragedy of civil war.

As was soon to be demonstrated the loyalty of the British Army itself could not be relied upon. The Daily Telegraph commented: "Any attempt to break the loyalists of Ulster by the armed forces of the Crown will probably result in the disorganisation of the Army for several years".

These foreboding words heralded another issue of grave concern for the tottering Liberal government. It finally erupted when whole cadres of British Army officers in Ireland, threatening serious disorder in Britain also should matters come to a head, refused to obey their government's orders if these involved dispositions or actions against the Unionists.

It did, indeed, come to a head, but, thanks to the manipulation amounting to genius of the Ulster-born Director of Military Operations, Major-General Henry Wilson, treasonable activity was confined to Ireland.

The situation had been increasingly explosive for some time. In Cork, (May, 1913) Alfred Lyttleton, M.P said – "It must be evident to everyone in Ireland, as it has become evident to everyone in England, that the present (Home Rule) Bill was not going to be forced through under the Parliament Act without bringing about the risk, which I think amounts to a certainty, of civil war... ".

---

[8] *The Strange Death of Liberal England*, G. Dangerfield, p. 110.

'Civil war is the path of danger, but it is also the path of duty; and I am convinced that no other alternative is left to the loyalists of Ulster', claimed Sir James Campbell, MP, in Swansea in March, 1914.

The so-called "Curragh Mutiny" occurred when, for the first time since 1688 elements of the British Army refused to act on its orders. Like much other community unrest and disruption threatening social if not military revolution in Britain at that time, such disorders were abruptly and unexpectedly diverted by events in far-off Sarajevo on June 28th, 1914, which would lead to astonishing changes throughout Europe in the next four years, in Ireland no less than anywhere else.

But it was primarily because of repeated challenges of this serious nature to the stability of Britain that, between March and August of 1914, the British government conceded more and more to the Unionists on the issue of Home Rule, not alone diluting further its already much weakened proposals (eventually amounted to little more than county council status), but amending them so that they excluded an undefined area of the Province of Ulster.

In February the collective, if idiosyncratically discrete, mind of the Liberal Cabinet was still cautious on the subject. Prime Minister Asquith threw a carrot to Redmond informing him that, in the interests of accord, he was prepared to grant the country control of its postal revenues and also local authority control. He evidently did so with that ineffable failure to understand any problem having its origin in a political context other than its own that is a hallmark of British administrators. He went on, however, to say that in order to offset these concessions (or perhaps the other way round), he also proposed to allow the Unionists to appeal against the application of Home Rule to Ulster, or some part of it.

Whatever Redmond's feelings may have been about this – and they are bound to have been less than enthusiastic – he made no significant protest.

Resulting also from the progressively ineffectual Home Rule proposals the British administration in Ireland adopted the view that they were only an interim body awaiting a transfer to a Home Rule administration under John Redmond who, increasingly, seems to have acted like a prime-minister-in-waiting, which may help explain some of his more curious behaviour.

A month later it was agreed that the Bill would include that Ulster would have the right to opt out of Home Rule for period of six years.

Thus the nose of partition, indeed like that of a scouting rodent, came to quiver on the frontiers of the constitutional hole it had nibbled and from which it would soon slither with a rustle that would echo resoundingly through the succeeding century.

This "soft option" of partition laid the foundations for what has tormented and bedevilled relations between the two countries ever since. One result was that, with the demise of Home Rule and the floating of partition, the first significant shift away from constitutional methods and towards an attempted military solution in twentieth century Ireland become more and more likely. On May 12[th,] 1914, Asquith announced that the Home Rule Bill would be passed through all stages, and that also he would simultaneously introduce an Amending Bill, the details of which he wisely refused to reveal.

War 1914-1918

On the outbreak of war, and in a master-stroke of political opportunism, Unionists, without abandoning their opposition to Home Rule, reaffirmed their allegiance to Britain. It was this, more than anything else, that ensured that the British Government not only "critically re-examined" its Home Rule policy – but did so with a view to securing the North and ensuring partition.

But it would be a mistake to think that the war and its consequences were the only major influences of profound and lasting change in Ireland that, at that time, brought about changes of shattering significance.

The profound social turmoil in Britain between 1910 and 1914 that resulted in rioting and a continuing series of major paralysing strikes, so rocked the Establishment there that talk of revolution, albeit a social one, was not uncommon. That this was so and that extraordinary events unthinkable less than a decade earlier should so seriously unsettle the normally unruffled and ordered pattern of life in middle-class Edwardian Britain, the government included, was a powerful indication of the increasing restlessness amongst the genuinely oppressed working classes.

It also reflected what was an even darker social situation in Ireland, one made all the more critical because of its alliance to genuine revolutionary thinking – perhaps best illustrated in a nutshell by the workers' Citizen Army which played a notable part from then until The Rising in 1916.

Under Captain Jack White, former British Army officer and son of Field Marshal Sir George White who relieved the siege of Ladysmith in the Boer war, the small, but efficient, Citizen Army had been formed, primarily as a workers' defence militia.

The social revolution that swept Europe in the preceding decade also enormously affected Ireland, encouraging urban populations, as had the Land League the rural, to an awareness of rights, until the rising clamour for social justice merged as a common *cri-de-coeur* from Irish workers with that for national self-determination.

In context these circumstances enable a better judgement to be made of the suggestion that Home Rule could have brought about what was achieved by the 1916 Rising and the War of Independence. It makes no sense. By August 1914 Home Rule was effectively dead, partition was on the way and, in Ireland, social and political justice seemed at best unlikely and at worst unattainable.

46

Ironically, it was Unionist opposition to Home Rule that contributed much to the erroneous notion that nationalists wanted nothing more. But, as we have seen, nationalism, particularly at its strongest, was by no means confined to the IPP. In reality the overall nationalist view of Home Rule, particularly once it was suspended and amended, was at best unenthusiastic and in general hostile. This was summed up by P.S. O'Hegarty as being:- "... dead and out of date. The political situation had changed materially both in Ireland and in England. In Ireland the Bill itself and the political theory behind it, that Irish self-government was something which England was entitled to give or to withhold, no longer commanded any support".[9]

Treason by the British Army

The so-called Curragh Mutiny in March 1914 by elements of the British Army remains one of the most extraordinary and under-noted events of the period. In effect Conservative Opposition, the highest levels of the British Army, the House of Lords – even a government minister – all, if in some cases peripherally, became involved in a treasonable and self-serving conspiracy against the government.

"The elderly lawyers who for the *most* part governed England ... were considerably startled at the prospect of an insurrection of peers, led by field-marshals and admirals, all pledged to sacrifice their lives in the cause of Ulster."[10]

The officer corps of the British Army, particularly of elite regiments came, almost without exception, from the landed or upper middle-classes with Tory backgrounds. Many were of Anglo-Irish Unionist families who, because of their

---

[9] P. S. O'Hegarty, *History of Ireland Under the Union, 1801-1922*, p. 744.

[10] Bulmer Hobson, *Ireland Yesterday and Tomorrow*, Tralee, 1968.

position, exercised in Ulster – indeed generally in the Ireland of the period - an influence out of all proportion to their numbers and real status; a kind of door-step colonialism.

A main conspirator was Major-General Sir Henry Wilson, a bigoted and convinced Ulster Unionist and an accomplished intriguer.

While recruiting was carried out openly in England, Scotland, and the English colonies for the purpose of controlling Irish Nationalists should the need arise, with paradox and hypocrisy flying about like autumn leaves in a wind-eddy, it comes as no surprise that Field Marshal Lord Wolseley should unburden himself of the remarkable observation that to use the army against any proposed Ulster insurrection "would be the ruin of the British army".

But it fell to a group of officers stationed at the Curragh in County Kildare to act. Some 60 of them resigned rather than, as they expressed it, be "forced to coerce Ulster". In this they were led and encouraged by their superiors in incredible conspiracy with the Director of Military Operations, General Wilson.

In March, 1914, the government sent orders to General Sir Arthur Paget, GOC British forces in Ireland to move troops to Armagh, Omagh, Enniskillen and Carrickfergus – the four strategic bases for military containment of Ulster. Paget affected to misunderstand his orders and instead moved stores.

On learning of the attitude of the generals in Ireland, Winston Churchill, then First Lord of the Admiralty, ordered two cruisers to Dublin Bay, two destroyers to Belfast Lough and a flotilla to the west coast of Scotland.

It is likely that the generals – probably with reason given developments in Europe - felt themselves to be in an invulnerable position. They almost certainly believed in the probability of a Conservative government soon taking office (what but a Conservative government would, after all, be capable of successfully pursuing a war for Britain?)

48

At this point a hitherto undistinguished brigadier by the name of H. de la P. Gough KCB, (descendant of the British field–marshal of the same name from Limerick who, in the interests of the then expanding British empire, had won his distinctions in what may fairly be described as globe-trotting wars against savages – otherwise the inhabitants of the places in which he had the misfortune to be), entered the scene. Having spoken with his commanding officer, Paget, the latter informed the British War Office by telegram as follows: "Officer commanding the 5th Lancers (Gough) states that all officers except two, and one doubtful, are resigning their commissions today. I much fear same conditions in 16th Lancers. Fear men will refuse to move." This was followed by a second telegram: "Regret to report, Brigadier and fifty-seven officers Third Cavalry Brigade prefer to accept dismissal if ordered North."

It was mutiny and Gough, commanding the Third Cavalry Brigade knew it. After the war he explained that his orders were either to undertake active operations or to leave the army, and that, in obedience to these orders, he decided to leave the army.

Another and totally unforeseen crisis, like some misbegotten genie from a concealed bottle, had now mushroomed to face the government from the Tory/Unionist misalliance. Any question of the government – and there had been some – now facing down the rebellious Ulster Unionists instantly evaporated.

Astonishingly, the army plot was supported by the Secretary for War, Colonel J. E. B. Seely, who met secretly with both Gough and Wilson in London and, rather than Seely having both men arrested for mutiny if not treason, between them they concocted a plan, the effect of which was that Gough and his officers walked away with a written guarantee that they would never have to operate against Ulster, *even if ordered to do so.*

The resulting uproar was calmed only when Asquith sacked Seely, and Generals Ewart and French, who had initialled the guarantee (a cosmetic exercise; they were rapidly reinstated on the outbreak of the impending war).

For the moment Asquith and his government had bought safety, in a situation in which the army had effectively dictated to it.

Like a tribe of ferocious Colonel Blimps, even to the quixotic extent of treason against Britain and possible civil war, Unionists claimed to stand for the Union with Britain, an eventuality closely perceived in Whitehall, which, as was its despotic habit, temporised.

Irish Nationalists, Volunteers and Sinn Fein were another matter. It was evident that the peasants were restless. Of all things, if you please, they demanded independence; there could be no question of temporising let alone compromise on that.

The Curragh incident also took the last question-mark out of partition. There would now be no question of Home Rule for Ulster. In a phrase of Churchill's "the Unionist minority barred the way to the rest of Ireland and now realised that they had a free hand to do as they liked".

The Unionists and the field generals of the Curragh in revolt against their government and supported by Wilson at the British War Office, had successfully and finally sabotaged even any limited prospect of Home Rule for Ireland as a whole.

Speaking in Bradford in March, 1914, Winston Churchill – who may be said to have had the interests of Great Britain rather than those of a sovereign Ireland closest to his energetic and percipient heart - summarised the position:-

"If Ulstermen extend the hand of friendship it will be clasped by Liberals and by their Nationalist countrymen in all good faith and in all good will; but if there is no wish for peace; if every concession that is made is spurned and exploited; if every effort to meet their views is only to be used as a means of breaking down Home Rule and of barring the way to the rest of Ireland; ... if the civil and Parliamentary systems under which we have dwelt so long,

50

and our fathers before us, are to be brought to the rude challenge of force ... and exposed to menace and brutality ...to disclose a sinister and revolutionary purpose ... then I can only say to you, 'Let us go forward together and put these grave matters to the proof.'"

So ended the Curragh Mutiny. Its effect had been profound.

Bachelor's Walk

In the name of Unionism there were already both a mutinous army and a treasonable "Government of Ulster" in the north of Ireland. Now a bloody event in Dublin was to underline harshly the different attitudes in Britain towards Unionists and Nationalists.

In 1914 the Irish Volunteers' lack of weaponry was seriously addressed for the first time, primarily through the unlikely aegis of a group of Anglo and Anglo-Irish sympathisers who, in contraposition to the mutineers of the British Army in Ireland, felt that if unarmed Volunteers were left to face the well-armed UVF in civil war the result would be slaughter.

The principal organisers of this arms plan were Roger Casement, Mrs. Alice Stopford Green, Mary Spring-Rice (daughter of Lord Monteagle), a Captain Berkeley and Erskine Childers and his wife.

The story of how the guns were bought in Germany and brought into Howth and Kilcoole in Wicklow is well-known.

When, after the guns had been landed at Howth, the Volunteers dispersed with their weapons between there and the North Strand as the British troops from the Royal Barracks marched back to Dublin onlookers jeered them.

Near O'Connell (then Sackville) street the British troops opened fire initially to disperse the unarmed crowd of jeering civilians.

When the justifiably enraged crowd armed themselves with stones and brick-bats and followed the soldiers the troops were ordered to fix bayonets. In Bachelor's Walk the British rearguard blocked the road and fired on the crowd, killing three people and wounding thirty-eight.

" ... if ever a slipshod killing deserved to be called 'massacre', the killing in Bachelor's Walk deserves that name. The comparisons between Larne and Howth are odious and revealing. At Larne 30,000 Orange rifles were landed while the police and coastguards and the soldiers slept: At Howth, the landing of 1,500 Nationalist rifles could only be expiated in blood... it matters very little whether three thousand civilians were slaughtered, or three hundred, or thirty, or three: there are stains in Bachelor's Walk which nothing will ever quite wash away...".[11]

The country reacted with shock and outrage. Recruits flocked to the Irish Volunteers, many being ex-soldiers, both officer and other-rank. But the suddenly swollen ranks of the Volunteers were to shrink again just as quickly following Redmond's recruitment speech for the British Army at Woodenbridge a few weeks later.

Confusion Compounded

In the extraordinary and uncertain situation, to become stirred to even greater confusion by the war, the IPP under John Redmond was both thoroughly confused and a significant player. It is clear that Redmond was increasingly out of touch with his electoral support[12]. It is also clear that the party itself, having committed itself to Home Rule, was beginning to feel the onset of that crisis of loyalty and identity that would eventually overwhelm it.

---

[11] Dangerfield, *op. cit., pp.420/1.*

[12] There were, and still are, those (including Dangerfield, op cit.) who accuse Redmond of being so much in love with the parliamentary procedures of Westminster that he was almost completely out of touch with his own electorate.

Nor was this at a political level only. Redmond's chief aide and confederate, John Dillon, pointed out to him what seems for a leader a somewhat trite and matter-of-fact point, namely that it was now a question of controlling or of being controlled. Principally because he had little other real choice, therefore, Redmond decided to make a take-over bid for the Irish Volunteers, of which, together with its women's auxiliary force, Cumann na mBan, he had up to then been dismissive and contemptuous.

As prime minister in waiting (possibly as Lord Redmond) and as leader of the IPP he was strenuously committed to the principle of Home Rule, even such a fractured, diminished and watered-down version as was then on offer. But he could not afford to ignore a nationalist armed militia such as the Volunteers; hence the "take-over bid", initially partially successful[13]. His followers (including former British servicemen) swelled the ranks of the Volunteers eightfold, an influx that, it was hoped, would provide a much-needed reservoir of experienced manpower. But it did not work out like that.

For reasons about which there was – and remains – speculation Redmond then did something quite extraordinary. It was, it must be remarked, a clear indication of his antiquated and unrealistic attitude attuned, it appears, more to the vanishing culture of a stylised British Edwardian drawing-room than to hard-knock parliamentarianism. It was, in fact, a glaring example of *cherchez la femme.*

The powerful – and to some notorious – London socialite and political hostess, Margot, wife of Prime Minister Asquith, whose habit it was to dabble in political intrigue, decided at this critical juncture to engage herself in Irish affairs.

A bare month before the outbreak of war, only days after the assassination of the Arch-Duke Ferdinand in Sarajevo,

---

[13]. In effect he demanded, and got, 50% representation on the Volunteer Council on foot of a threat to otherwise form a rival organisation.

and soon after his takeover of the Volunteers (his ultimatum to the Volunteers was on 9th June, 1914) she wrote to Redmond suggesting that he make "a great speech" and offer the Volunteers to the British Government in the event of war.

Austria was already at war and it was obvious that Germany and Russia would follow which meant that England and France would inevitably be embroiled. Irish affairs suddenly went on the back boiler of British political concerns as that country was overrun with patriotic fervour.

To Margot Asquith's letter Redmond, astonishingly, answered that he was very grateful for it and hoped that he might be able to follow her advice.

In the Commons he made a speech in the course of which, anticipating his Woodenbridge offer of Irish Volunteers to fight on the Continent, he stated that: "I say to the Government that they may tomorrow withdraw every one of their troops from Ireland. I say the coasts of Ireland will be defended from foreign invasion by her sons ..."

Within weeks and without prior consultation or discussion with those most involved, he took the extraordinary and unilateral step of urging the Volunteers to join the British Army and fight on the Continent as British troops against Germany.

This speech at Woodenbridge threw the Volunteer ranks, the original members of which were committed to Irish self-determination, into confusion. The recent influx of Redmondite supporters were Home Rulers to a man. An immediate split resulted and there were then two Volunteer forces where before Redmond's take-over there had been one. The Redmondite followers became the National Volunteers – and instantly and almost *en masse*, in response to Redmond's exhortations, marched to Flanders to become British cannon-fodder. The Irish Volunteers reverted in strength to much what they had been before Redmond's take-over, now no more.

Except that thousands of young Irishmen died needlessly fighting in the ranks of the British Army for a cause that was not theirs, Redmond's quixotic gesture was utterly wasted. What had happened? Why did he take such an extraordinary – one might say anti-national – course; what did he hope to achieve? The reality was probably unseen by him. He certainly did not acknowledge it. It was that even as his followers marched to battle in British uniforms, he and the IPP still relied – if uneasily - on the illusory principle of a political Gentleman's Agreement that Britain would stand over Home Rule for Ireland, under which the sands were already running and turning to quicksand.

Relations between the IPP and the separatists changed little over the next year and a half. The separatists included the increasingly politically active Sinn Fein (founded in 1905 by journalist Arthur Griffith as a nationalist party of passive resistance), the Volunteers, the secretive IRB and, by no means least, the influential cultural umbrella of the Gaelic League, the Gaelic Athletic Association (GAA), the Abbey Theatre and so on.

The IPP, confident in their way that, in time, "all would be for the best in the best of all possible worlds", did little else to further the cause of Home Rule, seeming content to leave it, and all it was supposed to achieve, in inanimate and indefinite suspension in the Statute Book of Westminster. It was clear, apart from the IPP's policy of do nothing and perhaps nothing will happen, that only they had the slightest faith left in Home Rule, and that was entirely of the blind variety. It would be reasonably accurate to say that as the prospect of Home Rule began to wither away in 1914, that of nationalist separatism waxed.

It is, therefore, not as surprising as it might seem that, as the IPP wavered, the Citizen Army under James Larkin and the socialist philosopher and power-house James Connolly, particularly the latter, became increasingly nationalist in outlook, combining a commitment to active separatism with its cooperative trades union socialist *raison d'etre*.

It is not uncommon today to hear the opinion that it was the Rising that pushed the Home Rule Bill to the British parliamentary back-boiler. That is a nonsense that ignores the fact that the porous version of Home Rule on the Statute book had been mortally crippled by 1914, let alone by the time of the 1916 Rising. The so-called Curragh mutiny alone – and there are other indicators – is ample demonstration of this.

Moreover, in considering the climate of the times, it is important to bear in mind that in Ireland general disquiet was strongly fuelled by the contempt with which the public felt they were being treated by the British parliament

Home Rule Interred

The stormy years from 1909 to 1914 that saw Asquith's Liberal government totter unsteadily through massive social upheaval into the war, and that roused the raw alliance of Tory and Unionist to march, like the Good Old Duke of York and his men, both up the stormy hill of revolt, and down again, also saw a powerful and sustained revitalisation of nationalism in Ireland.

We have seen that, no less than people elsewhere in Europe, the Irish were massively stimulated by social revolutionaries and land reformers in the train of Rosa Luxembourg and Michael Davitt, added to which the influence of the Volunteers, the IRB and the Citizen Army as well as the Celtic cultural dynamic, all contributed to a greater awareness of their worth as a nation and the (as yet unformed) willingness to do something about it. When faced with Britain's call to battle against Germany "for the rights of small nations", therefore, many Irish people had little difficulty in deciding that both the call and the shelving of Home Rule were no more than war-mongering and hypocrisy[14].

---

[14] Some writers and commentators, even one as distinguished as John Bruton (*The Irish Times, September 20th, 2004)*, report of

It was also an attitude that did not diminish their love and respect for those who, fuelled mainly by economic considerations, had gone – or were to go - to war in British uniforms. This, in the main, was simply an example of natural pragmatism. You eat, or you die; and if some have to die to eat, that is how, one way or another, it had been all through the previous century.

It was an outlook summarised by James Larkin in 1913, soon after the great Dublin strike, when he told a large English trades union audience that: "The Irish question is not a question of Home Rule. No, it is an economic question – a bread-and-butter question." There were, in reality, few illusions about Home Rule.

Thus we again return to our speculative claim. It is clear that to maintain that Home Rule had a prospect, at any time in the 20th century, of providing for Ireland what the 1916 Rising and the War of Independence subsequently helped bring about, is to cling to wishful thinking and, without adequate historical assessment or familiarity with the politics of the period, to blindly fly in the face of fact.

It was the Unionists, not the Nationalists, who exploded in opposition to Home Rule, who forced its emasculation; who reintroduced armed and organised revolt and – from the British point of view – treason into the politics of the period, and who precipitated the Cyclopean crisis that overwhelmed the country and fatally crippled the Liberal Party in England - doing all but the same to the British Tory Party that had unleashed the tiger in the first place.

The Tory perception of the Liberal Government was of a libertine agent that would sacrifice the empire, including Ireland, on the altar of liberalism. But no sooner was the Beast that they chose to fight this perceived threat unleashed, than the tail of that Unionist Behemoth, with what seemed to be uncontrollable violence, started to wag the Tory

---

address to the Reform Movement which advocates rejoining the Commonwealth have difficulty with this.

constitutionalist dog (such as it was), hurling it violently towards destruction of the Tory structure itself and towards civil war in Ireland, and possibly even in Great Britain.

It was both an irony and a deliverance that the war came to diffuse and deflect this tense and astonishing situation.

Faced with conflicting choices, neither of which would easily go away, the British Government had quite simply been reprieved by the war. Nevertheless the reality, unpalatable though it may be to some, is that the Home Rule Bill had already been so disabled before the outbreak of war that it served little Irish interest.

Even if – and there are many "ifs" – there had been no rebellion two years on in 1916; no overwhelming defeat by Sinn Fein of the Irish Parliamentary Party in 1918; if the Government of Ireland Act of 1920 had not been introduced giving Northern Ireland a separate – and ideologically sectarian - identity and government and a putative, non-mandated one, for the south; and even if Home Rule *had* been introduced after the war, it would not, and could not have provided the elements of sovereignty that were in the Agreement of 1921 that was the Treaty.

Confirmation, if needed, as discernable and eloquent as a blast of flame, comes in the words of Carson himself who, on the introduction of the Amending Bill (July 8th 1914) excluding fiscal autonomy and all nine counties of Ulster from the original Home Rule provisions, declared Home Rule now to be "a nullity".

And, indeed, it was; a constitutional corpse wrapped in a shroud of suspense sliding, silent and unremarked, beneath the turmoil of war that roared over it.

Never again would the finger of Home Rule be lifted to point towards the political structure of Ireland. It was, like the edge water of an ebb tide on a sandy beach, slowly disappearing from sight.

Major considerations in 1914 were Britain's strategic and industrial resources. Belfast was the only significant industrial city in Ireland and, so far as critical shipbuilding was concerned, it was of major importance. From the British war-cabinet point of view, therefore, appeasement on partition had profound practical aspects.

In effect the options were:-

1. Concede the Home Rule Bill and face the rebellious wrath of the Unionists, also putting at risk war-time strategic interests, or

2. Further dilute and amend the Home Rule Bill, appease the Unionists and, to that extent, secure those interests.

At the same time appearances were necessary and, as a consequence and as we have seen, the Bill was suspended for the duration of the war and for as long thereafter as might be thought necessary, further amended to include a partitioned, but undetermined, area - that would certainly include Belfast – of the north of Ireland and fiscal and other limitations.

In keeping with the imperialistic outlook then still informing many colonial rulers and ruled alike, the attitude of perplexed British leaders appears to have been that they were in fact being constitutionally benevolent towards the Irish. They were, after all, proposing to confer political and administrative "liberties" in keeping with policies of "freedom, education and enlightenment" on them. That the Irish demanded more was frustrating and inexplicable. In return for these – generous – semi-autonomous favours and benefits all they asked was recognition of and loyalty to Britain's acknowledged mighty role and status in the world. If there were also questions of contributing to Britain's coffers at their own expense and to British cannon-fodder, that was only right and proper and as it should be.

Some may have recognised the inherent injustice, but they remained quite disingenuous in ignoring it.

All this, of course, was deeply and increasingly resented in Ireland as the sense of national identity, hurled into troubled slumber by the Great Famine and its consequences, reawakened. A striking (if, with hindsight, apparently modest), effect between 1914 and 1916 was the switch in

Irish political focus from the futile Home Rule proposals to, increasingly, that of re-establishing national sovereignty.

Less well known and ultimately of far greater importance, were the negotiations by Casement and both Plunketts, the Count and his son Joseph, with the German High Command in Germany in 1914/15/16.

But consideration of them properly belongs to our second myth and we will leave that fascinating aspect of early 20th century Irish politics, which it affected so profoundly to the second essay, where it properly belongs.

Meantime, to complete our examination of Home Rule so quickly absorbed by the sands of history's fickle ebb-tide, it is enough to say that after 1916 there was no further mention of Home Rule at all.

When the 1918 general election astonished Britain by wiping out the IPP, in returning the "Shinners" in great numbers and in providing a base for a national – if proscribed – Irish parliament (Dail Eireann), the British Government reacted with the speed, determination and focus that surfaces when British interests are visibly threatened and that, for centuries, have been outstanding characteristics of that imperial structure. The partitionist Government of Ireland Act of 1920 was very quickly, prepared, approved and enacted.

The sequence of historical events itself indicates that Home Rule would have benefited the country little, if at all. The suggestion that it would have produced the same results as were achieved by the Rising of 1916 and the War of Independence flies in the face of reality.

Here is the relevant sequence we have considered:-

1. Before the autumn of 1914 the proposed Home Rule Bill providing for limited autonomy for all-Ireland, by then systematically reduced from its original intent and on the British Statute book, was further restricted. An Amending Bill provided for partition (an undetermined portion of Ulster, generally expected to be the whole province), additional restrictions,

including no fiscal autonomy, were introduced, together with indefinite suspension of the Act itself.

2. Notwithstanding counter propaganda the 1916 Rising achieved most of what it intended – namely proclaiming the republic, reviving nationalist separatist fervour, creating the conditions necessary for a hearing before the post-war peace-conference as then conceived and in accordance with Germany's undertaking to that effect.

3. Sinn Fein's overwhelming destruction of the IPP in the 1918 general election, repeated in that of 1921, ended any lingering and unlikely prospect for Home Rule or that the IPP – or any incarnation of it – might take power.

4. Britain's 1920 Government of Ireland Act marked the grave of Home Rule.

It was not simply Home Rule versus Sinn Fein's aspirations that was the issue. During the years 1914-1918 Home Rule was just the exhausted aspiration of a political party – the IPP - in the process of being interred. The party leader was so out of touch with the people and with the dynamic motivating so many of them that, like a fairy-tale bad baron penalised with blindness, he tapped about with his cane searching for the "stuff that dreams are made on", long after it had, like the citizens themselves, gone elsewhere.

Some "*revisionistas*", mainly by manipulating those most insubstantial and malleable of all sources of information, statistics, tried to show that Sinn Fein's electoral victory was less comprehensive than it was. It is difficult to understand the point they seek to make. No matter how one carves it up the Irish Party was demolished and Sinn Fein took 80% of the seats – and did even better in the 1921 election. One would have thought that the facts speak loudly enough for themselves.

But, in the address already mentioned, stating that "Ireland would have achieved independence without 1916", John Bruton went on to maintain that it was "very much open to argument whether all that was achieved –" in terms of independence and sovereignty "- could *[not]* have been achieved without a single shot being fired".

At this point we might also legitimately ask: Why do advocates of this ephemeral Home Rule theory always stop dead at such "independence" it might have achieved "if only" or "supposing"?

What is supposed to have happened next?

In a cogent summary Mr. Pat Burke stated the reality: "without an armed struggle 'southern Ireland' would have remained an integral part of the United Kingdom of Great Britain and Ireland –"[15].

In that event the following would have been virtually certain:

Ireland would, willy-nilly, have been plunged into the Second World War with enormous loss of life and property relative to its population and development;

The Sinn Fein, Volunteer and IRB movements would not have gone away and, sooner or later, a major and popular attempt in arms to achieve full and independent sovereignty would certainly have again taken place - possibly during the course of World War Two (with all the hypothetical woeful consequences entailed).

There would have been no Celtic Tiger or much else in the way of economic progress and, lastly Ireland's relationship with the EU would now be very different and less significant.

To so distort fact and manipulate reality in order to try to give substance to an historical blank is nonsensical. To seek to elevate such a chimera to the level of reality does a grave and ignoble disservice to all those who, selflessly and with no motive other than to accomplish sovereignty in the name of the people, devoted themselves to that end. A moment's reflection demonstrates the absurdity of this. As Garrett

---

[15] The Irish Times, 22nd September 2004.

FitzGerald wrote recently: "That Home Rule would lead to independence is alternative history gone mad."

Briefly and in conclusion the significance of the 1918 election results was not lost on either the British or Irish leaderships. Sinn Fein reorganised the institutions of nationalism under common political, constitutional, leadership at its Ard Fheis in 1919 when the Republic, declared in 1916, was reaffirmed and a new government, Dail Eireann, the first popular native Irish government in modern history, was constituted from elected representatives.

In Britain Sinn Fein's success was viewed differently. The overwhelming defeat of the IPP had not been anticipated. Its virtual disappearance from Westminster dramatically upset the balance of power, while the emergence of a powerful and unified separatist and organised political structure in Ireland was totally unforeseen. They rushed to take "appropriate action" - the result being the Government of Ireland Act that remains the legal and constitutional basis for partition. It approved two Home Rule style parliaments – a northern, in effect "a Protestant parliament for a Protestant people" in Ulster, sitting in Belfast – and a southern parliament for the rest of Ireland, sitting in Dublin.

They were not parliaments in the sense of being representative or democratic or having any significant autonomy, being subordinate to Westminster in all but local administration.

The northern assembly was formally opened by King George of England on 22nd June 1921. The southern parliament, boycotted (to use an interesting word in this context) by all but the four *ex officio* members from Dublin University (Trinity College), met briefly, after which these four members simply dispersed. It never met again.

The defeat of Germany in 1918 meant that Irish hopes of a hearing, let alone a sympathetic one, at the Versailles Peace conference, were also defeated. Nevertheless Dail Eireann sent emissaries led by Sean T. O Kelly, later to be the second

President of Ireland, to try to obtain recognition from the victors.

But the opposition to Irish aspirations was overwhelming. It goes without saying that Britain was opposed to any question of entitlement by Ireland. Woodrow Wilson, President of the United States, a dyed in the wool WASP with an Ulster background, refused his support. In spite of Ireland's long association with France, Georges Clemenceau, "The Tiger", President of France and of the Peace Conference, and the most vehemently anti-German of all the Allied leaders, also refused his support, possibly because the Irish sought help from Germany and that the 1916 Proclamation referred to "gallant allies in Europe".

Meantime another factor entered the Irish/British arena – the War of Independence, underway since 1919.

Both sides were then locked in a struggle at two levels in Ireland – political or constitutional and military.

Well telegraphed in advance the 1920 Act was welcomed in the north, except in Catholic areas – a minimum of 40% of any proposed area. Voices in Britain generally proclaimed it a just solution provided by the Mother of Parliaments for an intractable people. Home Rule was now laid to official rest.

But the intractable people of what the British now termed Southern Ireland, and whose expressed wishes were ignored in this divisive Act, were outraged and rejected it holus-bolus.

A turbulent and anomalous situation then existed in Ireland. It was legislatively partitioned by Britain along sectarian lines, with a functioning, Unionist, modified Home Rule-type government in (an as yet undefined area of) northern Ireland. Another nominal, but non-functional, government was legislated for in southern Ireland where the old British administration continued to operate from Dublin Castle. Dail Eireann, the elected government of the people, though proscribed by the British, functioned with established Courts of Justice responsible to its authority. The War of Independence intensified.

Official British terror tactics were introduced in the shape of the Black and Tans, Auxiliary police cadets ("Auxies") and certain army units. Much of the country was subject to Martial Law and brutal methods of suppression and intimidation were employed against Volunteers and the civil population, alike.

Curiously the argument is also sometimes heard that the Irish were wrong to engage in guerrilla war with the British forces occupying the country. It is a foolish and specious argument of no merit either historically or as propaganda, similar to saying that the French, the Czechs, the Poles and so on were wrong for acting in the same way against occupying forces in their countries.

From the British perspective, of course, it looked different. We should bear in mind that when the First World War began imperialism was the almost universal political/economic system in the developed civilised world, expansionist America with her eyes and hands already plundering the Pacific and the Caribbean not excepted.

There were only two major republics in the world, France and the United States. Economic clientism enriched the great imperial powers while simultaneously holding their dependent nations in economic – and often physical – thrall.

And the First World War became in essence – whatever it may have been initially - a power-struggle between 19th century-style, *laissez-faire* based empires, and free-trade nationalism of one kind or another.

So astonishingly far-reaching, however, was the power of change and the vision of the common man that when the war ended after a mere four years of bloody conflict, five mighty empires and some lesser ones, had gone – the Russian, the Austro-Hungarian, the German, the Chinese and the Ottoman; the Belgian and the Dutch. A sixth, the British, was shaken and close to bankruptcy.

In the face of this astonishing reality, the turning of the world as it had been known and had developed for more than 200 years on its head, the very last thing the British wanted was the disintegration of their own empire – in particular that bit of it that was its oldest and most strategically placed colony on its Atlantic doorstep.

It had taken more than 300 years to make Ireland tractable, or at least to unite it under the Act of Union with Great Britain. Strategic and economic interests far outweighed the price of controlling the strangely restive and unruly Irish.

The country stood as a bulwark between Britain and the open Atlantic. It simply was not in Britain's interests that control of the island should pass from her hands. There were also substantial economic reasons why that should not happen; unskilled manpower for various purposes; so long as its wages and prices were kept low and her agricultural produce restricted to and available to the British market at close to cost-price, Ireland was a convenient source of cheap food for the increasing British population; her native industries had been stifled so she offered little challenge to British industry. Her contribution in man-power from time-to-time to Britain's various war efforts was most convenient and useful.

That, or variations on it, pretty well encompassed the average British person's view of the situation.

At just what point the British Government realised that further coercion would not work is unclear, but realise it at some point – almost certainly following the 1918 election - they did.

In spite of this Britain continued for three years to suppress, by orthodox and unorthodox military force, the fight for independence.

As always the prime objective was Britain's best interests and to that the answer was clear; minimum concessions and maximum retention at both strategic and economic levels. On balance the actual level of concessions was a relatively simple matter of negotiation to concede as little as possible so long as Northern Ireland was secure, the (then) strategically significant Atlantic ports were secure; war,

66

pension and other indemnities were met and some political restrictions put in place together with the costs of the concessions allowed. Abstract principle had nothing to do with the British position except in so far as they might take advantage of the Irish attitude to it.

Accordingly the question of terms was considered along such lines.

The Irish, infinitely less experienced in such matters, while disposed to terms, saw things differently.

The outcome was the Treaty which brought sovereignty to more than three-quarters of the country. The northeast was excluded under the terms of the 1920 Act.

So why does this empty argument about Home Rule, more appropriate to the voice of moribund imperialism, still persist and chirp meaninglessly in Ireland like the cricket in the hearth across the voice of historical reality?

It is a shadow thing, a Will o' the Wisp; the wishful thinking of those who squint through the mournful "if only" hedges of history looking for what might have been, but never was.

The most reliable contemporary sources were satisfied that Home Rule as a functional resolution of Irish political affairs was moribund by 1914, and dead before either 1916 or the War of Independence took place. The facts of history overwhelmingly confirm this opinion. There is no evidence of any kind that Home Rule would have – or, indeed, could have – achieved anything other than the threatened civil war between Unionists and Nationalists. What the outcome of such catastrophe might have been is probably best left to the Home Rule theorists to conclude.

Anyone who glances through the Home Rule provisions and compares them with those of the Treaty cannot fail to see that Home Rule did not permit fiscal autonomy, which the Treaty did; it did not permit a national Defence Force, which the Treaty did; it did not permit sovereign status, which the Treaty did (if initially in a modified form) and so on.

In short Home Rule did not provide, and could not have provided, the same freedoms as were achieved by 1916 and the War of Independence and to argue otherwise is a nonsense. Nevertheless it is a remarkable fact that some people still hold strong feelings about Home Rule evidently because it is something they inexplicably *want* to believe in.

THE SECOND MYTH

Playing False With 1916

THE SECOND MYTH

Playing False With 1916

NOTWITHSTANDING ANY TENDENCY to believe only what is convenient, the dismissal of the pivotal and formative event of modern Irish history as a wrong-headed, pointless and romantic "Blood-sacrifice" is very bizarre. This dismissal flies so questionably and so pointedly in the face of the facts that its very existence demands explanation as well as correction.

The answer to why the Easter Rising of 1916 (generally known in Ireland as "The Rising") is distorted and misrepresented in this way is – to be contradictory about it - fairly straightforward; may, at first glance, even appear simplistic. And that, in fact, is part of the reason for its success. It is, in a nutshell, and as will be demonstrated, the result of clever and durable Black Propaganda.

The Rising was the single most important event in Irish national and sovereign development for the past two hundred years. As a seminal idea it germinated in the republican rising of 1798. It matured as the Easter Rising into an active and profoundly formative ideal.

Even at this remove the period 1910 to 1922 is still subject to mythologizing – often the residue of that hostile "Black propaganda".

Of course 1916 was "a protest in arms". But it was also much more, going beyond any basic military or political purpose - one reason, perhaps, why it can be difficult to define and why the distorted version persists.

First and foremost the Rising was a *revendication*, that is a claim to the indefeasible right - which can not be forfeited - of the sovereign nature of the country and the people. It set out to endow the people with a transformation of public attitude and perception greater than any since the Union with Great Britain was foisted on the country in 1801.

Often – perhaps most often – The Rising is looked on as if it happened unexpectedly and in isolation. Such was far from being the case. It was not only very much of its time and place, it was a long-term objective that had awaited opportunity and was, specifically, the result of careful and detailed planning over the previous nineteen or twenty months by the IRB.

To imagine that the constitutional/separatist pendulum affecting Irish political outlook, behaviour and manners throughout the 19th century diminished or went away in 1900 with the new century would be a serious mistake. The rickety bridge of Home Rule spanned the notional gap between the centuries and, while there was some confusion when it died, although the uneasiness of the people was quite different to the apathy of ten or twelve years earlier and from the social agitation of a few years previously, there was also a revived national energy resulting in part from dissatisfaction and a growing sense of betrayal with the IPP. Political energy began to focus more strongly – if as yet modestly - on what was collectively, and incorrectly, dubbed Sinn Fein activity.

Yet there was an uninformed truth in this integral label since the Volunteers, the Citizen Army, trades unions, the

GAA, the Gaelic League - Sinn Fein itself - and other social groups had all been infiltrated by the IRB, so that together they formed part of the developing recipe that would eventually provide the drive for nationalism, separatism and change.

On the outbreak of War the IRB decided that a Rising would take place and it duly did (the War of Independence, between 1919 and 1921, which was supported by the vast majority of the people, also had its origins in this decision). By 1914 Home Rule was dead and the political theory behind it (that Irish self-government was something which England was entitled to give or to withhold), died with it. Accordingly, to the question: Could what 1916 achieved - proclamation of the Republic and a resurgence of nationalist spirit - have been achieved by Home Rule, the answer is quite simply "No".

The nationalist physical force programme was not the only driving force that led to the prism of 1916. In the early years of the 20th century social revolution had been clamorous and violent all across Europe. In Ireland, between 1911 and 1914, formidable labour movements organising and activating workers, encouraged a powerful awareness of human and social rights that expressed itself at several levels throughout those heady years.

We have already noted that some commentators on the Rising claim that 1916 did not have a social dimension. The grounds on which this claim is based are seldom stated. It may be, as is increasingly the case, that they apply today's standards to that time, a meaningless exercise from which no valid conclusions can be drawn.

The reality is that in addition to being an armed uprising of nationalist purpose the Rising was also a response to James Larkin's clarion-call to "The Risen People".

The Proclamation of the Republic makes its social dimension clear. But it was James Connolly, the trades union leader and active socialist, proposing to act independently with his Citizen Army if the Irish Volunteers failed to do so, who, in

January 1916, brought matters to a head. And it was his small Citizen Army, composed of trade-unionists, that would have acted with him had he gone it alone[16].

To suggest that Connolly's thinking, acting, preparation and planning of the Rising did not include a social dimension is ludicrous.

It is also curious – and clearly also propaganda - that while the bravery of those taking part in the Rising is acknowledged, their military planning and ability is frequently derided (notably seldom if ever by military authorities). The theory goes that the Rising was an inept military adventure without hope of success dreamed up and executed by an irresponsible and romantic group of visionaries and poets in what was called a "blood sacrifice" – thereby also establishing an improbable link with the events of Easter. Those who pursue this trendy iconoclastic role of dragging down the great disparage and sneer at them and their achievements without one shred of evidence in support of their views.

The above theory, which so distorts and misrepresents both The Rising and those who took part in it, has been particularly prevalent since the mid 1960s. The facts, the DNA of history, are writ. But fact and reality were, for a time, swept aside in the 1970s and 1980s during a plague of uncritical, so-called, revisionism become an end in itself.

This distortion of the concept of "blood-sacrifice" was particularly directed at Padraic Pearse.

Of the distortions Irish history has been subjected to this, grounded on the premise that its leaders were incompetent and wrong and The Rising one of despair for a hopeless

---

[16] In a curious contradiction to his assertion that The Rising did not have a social dimension, Michael Hopkinson also maintains:- "However, Irish revolutionary socialism was never to recover from the intellectual and charismatic leadership of James Connolly…" (*The Irish War of Independence,* p.13 *)* evidently overlooking, or forgetting, that it was in fact Connolly who forced the issue of the Rising – not once, but twice.

cause, is one of the most deplorable. It diminishes The Rising and denigrates those who took part in it. Part of this approach appears to be based on the argument that we need new, revised thinking on 1916 in order to see the reality – possibly even on the basis that an historical study of the period will not be noteworthy unless it has something new and controversial to say.

It is certainly right and proper that entrenched perceptions of historical events should, from time to time, be re-examined. But 'revision' as an end in itself and in which historical events are judged in contemporary terms, is bombast. The facts of history don't work like that.

But, even on the positive side, there is a fundamental flaw in the common version of The Rising. Most books and articles written during the past 20 years about it contain the assumption that the Volunteers fought the British forces in Ireland in the hope – even in the prospect – of achieving some kind of military victory.

Even to the least military minded it should not take more than a moment's reflection to appreciate that the idea of a military victory by the Volunteers over the British Army in Ireland is preposterous. At no time was any such hope, prospect or intent part of the IRB/Volunteer plan. Commentators sometimes try to overcome the inherent nonsense in this by relying on the conclusion that if it was not intended to achieve military victory then the only other possible alternative is that it was the mythical 'blood sacrifice'.

While this thesis is essentially in contradiction of the doctrine of "blood-sacrifice", many revisionists with sublime illogicality nevertheless manage to hold both these views.

Incredible though it may be, this is often paraded as dogmatic fact:- "To take over prominent buildings, and at that not the most appropriate ones, to set up a hopelessly-confused plan of operations with Germany, America and the provinces, and not even to block the communication route for British reinforcements from Kingstown to the centre of

Dublin, were all to invite disaster. Apart from its slipshod planning, the Rising demonstrated the absurdity of nineteenth-century notions of romantic revolution at a time of huge advances in military technology. To virtually court the execution, or at least imprisonment, of the leadership and to potentially decimate the fighting forces were strange ways to expect to win a war"[17].

---

[17] It is laughably noticeable that some academics seem to think that they are also skilled military tacticians and have no hesitation in pontificating thereon, often ludicrously. In this typically distorted view of the Rising Dr. Hopkinson (*op. cit*, p.13*)* includes some curious military observations. With the possible exception of St. Stephen's Green, which in any case was occupied by the Citizen Army, the positions occupied by the Volunteers were, in the opinions of military experts who have studied them, excellent, chosen with military and tactical skill. "The decision to ...[use]... the large buildings of Dublin was sound, because this ... favours the defenders who are generally the weaker force. This method of warfare was favourable to the Insurgents and their mission as no other could be on Easter Monday 1916", Maj. Gen. (then Col.) P. J. Halley, *The Irish Sword*, Vol. VII, No. 29, Winter, 1966. At a lecture in Trinity College in 2006 Professor Charles Townshend castigated the Volunteers for not occupying more buildings – specifically Dublin Castle, Trinity College, the Bank of Ireland and other outposts - it was pointed out that this was not feasible since less than one third the anticipated muster had mobilised and that, therefore, what was intended to be garrisoned by, say, 60 men could only be occupied by 20 and that to reduce units at one third strength to further inadequately man other posts was not a good idea and that the Volunteers did the only practical thing, shortened their perimeter and tried to concentrate and extend their field of fire. His response to this was: -"I disagree!" In discussing the proposed withdrawal by the Dublin Volunteers to the Shannon Townshend observed that it was an utterly stupid plan since, he said quite correctly, a withdrawal under attack from superior forces is one of the most difficult military manoeuvres.

Typically this paragraph puts an utterly false construction on The Rising. The 1916 planners were no more stupid about military matters than anybody else – some were very expert.

While such comments may be based on unsuspected command and staff ambitions (by no means evident here) they serve only to obliterate reality. With the possible exception of St. Stephen's Green, occupied by the Citizen Army, the positions occupied by the Volunteers, in the opinions of military experts such as General P. J. Halley and An Col. Eoghan O Neill who have studied them, were chosen with military and tactical skill.

It is, perhaps, worth listing some points:-

i/ The plan of operations was well thought out and militarily sound in relation to its purpose. It will be considered later.

ii/ The Rising was not, and was never intended to be, a revolution, romantic or otherwise.

iii/ The buildings designated for take-over as strong-points with outposts in Dublin during the Rising were, within the scope of the plan, strategically and tactically excellent.

But the reason Broadstone, Westland Row and Kingsbridge stations were to be held was to enable a withdrawal *by rail*; moreover, other than an undermanned artillery park at Athlone, there were few if any troops between Dublin and the Shannon. It took until Friday before the British were able to muster a force of 100 marines to seek the Connacht Volunteers. There seems to be no tactical reason why the originally planned withdrawal to the Shannon would not have succeeded.

17a Professor Joe Lee got it right: "In the event, the Rising had turned into a blood sacrifice. But it had not been planned that way from the outset ... however profusely blood sacrifice sentiments spatter the later writings of Pearse and MacDonagh, and however retrospectively relevant they appeared to be in the circumstances, it seems unhistorical to interpret these sentiments as the basis of the actual planning of the Rising..." op.cit. pp 25/6.

As to how, even with the entire Volunteer force mustered, the routes (two were in use) between Dublin and 'Kingstown' could have been blocked in order to prevent incoming British reinforcements in division strength from reaching Dublin, does raise an interesting tactical and logistical question. The answer would surely be of considerable interest to most military colleges.

On the other hand the story of the Volunteers' well-chosen blocking strong-point at Mount Street Bridge has gone down in history.

It must – or at least it should – be evident from even cursory knowledge of the facts that the leaders of The Rising had no intention of throwing either the lives of the Volunteers or their own lives away in some kind of worthless gesture, as Pearse's cease-fire order emphasises.

It is regrettable that this lingering propaganda, rather than the important and comprehensive reality, is still so often peddled as the common view of the Rising. Indeed it is more than merely regrettable when it is added to such nonsense as:-"the principle behind hunger-striking corresponded with Pearse's blood-sacrifice ideology"[18].

Where did this insidious "blood sacrifice" smoke-screen phrase come from and why does it linger?

It appeared soon after the event at a time when the ruthless and percipient military intelligence arm of a hostile and enraged Britain, the clever brain-child of the then neophyte MI6 was anxious to make an establishing impact. Like all good propaganda it not only misrepresents the truth - it does so in a convincing and credible manner. Moreover it has been given clever phantom support from isolated lines of verse by a few of the 1916 leaders.

Again a moment's reflection will make it obvious that if everyone's actions and motives, including those of readers, were determined by some odd lines of verse taken out of context that they may have written from time to time, our

---

[18] Hopkinson, *op.cit.*

opinions of others and theirs of us would be very strange indeed.

The reality is that 1916 was a well-planned and calculated strategy formulated with every prospect of achieving its objectives. Even though it did not develop fully as intended it gained all except one of these objectives. As it was it succeeded spectacularly with two out of the three, and did not succeed with the third only because it was outside its control to do so, failing through no fault of the plan or of the planners.

Background

Before 1916 the comprehensive nationalist movements including the Home Rule movement, Sinn Fein and the Volunteers, the trades union movement with its own armed force the Citizen Army, and the IRB - secretive, masterful of intrigue, and patient in the old Fenian tradition, the hidden hand behind both the formation of the Irish Volunteers in 1913 and the planning of the Rising - were increasingly active. All except the Home Rule movement, tended to converge towards a common nationalist stream.

This Irish/Ireland ethos, as it might be called, was also fuelled by the Irish social and cultural movements that also cross-fertilised with the above and with each other and permeated all levels of society – the Gaelic Athletic Association, the Gaelic League, the Land League, and other cultural movements.

While it was in no sense a decisive factor this expansive support for Irish nationalism can only have had the effect of reassuring the Military Council in its preparations of active – as opposed to contingency or opportunist – plans for a rising.

While these developments strengthened opposition to Home Rule had already, as we have seen, led to treason and near civil war in the north of Ireland.

The question to be asked is – Why are the men and women who, suddenly and unexpectedly splintered the gates of the last surviving European empire in the space of mere months and in the name of Irish self-determination - so often and wrongfully lied about and demeaned so that their own people and inheritors are wrongly influenced by such distortions?

There can not be many states where mindless prejudice so distorts the memories of its patriot founding fathers, or where the public in general is so saturated with falsehood that it is falsehood rather than fact that is believed.

Plans for the Rising began within days of the 4th of August declaration of war by England against Germany, when the Supreme Council of the IRB met in the Gaelic League building, 25 Parnell Square, Dublin, and took three crucial decisions.

The first was straightforward; preparations should be made for a rising i/ if a German Army invaded Ireland; ii/ if England attempted to enforce conscription on Ireland and, iii/ if the war looked like ending and a rising had not yet taken place [19]. As we know under the terms of the 1873 decision by its Council an IRB Provisional Government of Ireland already existed.

The second decision was to seek whatever help was possible from Germany, and the third was to create a military council to plan the Rising. When the council was formed it was charged to "prepare an insurrection and secure control of the Volunteers". Its first members included Pearse, Joseph Plunkett and Eamon Ceannt.

"To secure control of the Volunteers. . ." the statement of purpose is clear and specific.

From the perspective of a comfortable place in a twenty-first century sovereign state, it is often far from easy to grasp the temper of an Ireland in the early years of the twentieth.

---

[19] In any event "we should rise in revolt, declare war on England and, when the conference was held to settle the terms of peace, we should claim to be represented as a belligerent nation." Sean T. O Ceallaigh, *An Phoblacht*, April 1926.

Contrary to what may be described as a simplistic – if prevalent – conclusion, it needs to be emphasised that the decision for a rising against the English occupation does not mean, and should not be interpreted as meaning, that it would be either along 'blood-sacrifice lines, or that any prospect of military victory was envisaged. The Volunteers allowed for some military success, but overall military victory was not, and never could have been, an objective of The Rising. The Volunteers numbered about 18,000 men of whom some 2,000 were also members of the IRB, and tended to be officers dominating the Volunteer command structure, thus facilitating control. Arms were in very short supply.

It has been argued that the Rising was a *coup de main* by the IRB on the unsuspecting Volunteers, especially in Headquarters. That ignores the fact that the Volunteers, to begin with, were the creation of the IRB with the intention of using them for precisely this purpose.

The Rising was planned by the Military Council in the closest secrecy, unknown even to Volunteer officers often sharing HQ duties, responsibilities and directorates with them.

For these and other reasons it is clear that looking backwards with self-validating argument and myopic hindsight so as to maintain that, because it fails to conform to contemporary certainties, the Rising was wrong and misguided simply emphasises that this thoughtless procedure is arguing backwards – *a posteriori.*

In fact three independent organisations, one way or another, were preparing for a rising in the years before 1916. They were the Volunteers, the IRB and the Irish Citizen Army. It is clear from Connolly's writings that if the IRB/Volunteers had not moved he and his small Citizen Army would have. Since, so far as we know, the Citizen Army had no strategic plan and little hope of even a sustained fight, a Rising by them on their own would, indeed, have been more in the nature of a forlorn hope. But, MacNeill's rejection notwithstanding it can hardly be doubted that if they had decided to go it alone, the IRB and the Volunteers would have come to their support. But that situation did not arise and the reason, a matter of strategy and timing by all three organisations, is clear and dramatic.

Joseph Plunkett was held in high esteem as a pragmatic military expert. He was a member of the IRB and the Military Council (also known as the Military Committee, who were also all ranking Volunteer officers), engaged, since 1914, in planning The Rising.

The German ambassador in Washington, Count von Bernsdorff and the first secretary, Wolf von Igel, were also involved in the planning as was John Devoy of the US based Clan na Gael. But most vital to Irish plans was the agreement and participation of the authorities in Germany, particularly the Foreign Office, the General Staff and the Admiralty, represented by Count Bethmann Hollweg, Count Nadolny and Captain Heydal respectively. They negotiated with Plunkett in Berlin in 1915 and were all involved in the preliminary planning. Last, but by no means least, were Captain Karl Spindler of the *Aud* and Roger Casement, who had been instrumental in organising the Howth gun-running and who went to Germany soon after the outbreak of war in 1914.

Casement's involvement – distorted, misrepresented and misunderstood – was to become a matter of profound significance in the aftermath of the Rising. Because of what, rightly or wrongly, is alleged to have been his excessive romanticism, he was discounted – even distrusted, but used where useful - by some of his fellow conspirators. A notable exception was his experienced military advisor Robert Montieth. But, in turn, the IRB, Devoy in America and the German authorities appear to have decided that he was too romantic and unreliable - a conclusion, it must be said, that affected Irish/German relations and plans for the Rising at a critical time.

The German General Staff, initially enthusiastic, developed reservations about the Irish proposals. Amongst other things these reservations are said to have been because of the enormous demands on German resources when the French not only held their great - and intended to be decisive - onslaught at Verdun, but unexpectedly counterattacked. This did not, however, mean - and it is a small, but independent, measure of the thoroughness and validity of the Irish plan that it was so – that the Germans abandoned the Irish, even in their own unexpected crisis.

Two main factors appear to have governed the German attitude. The first was strategic; the extent, if any, to which an Irish uprising would benefit the German war effort, and, secondly, their confidence in the Irish to conduct a successful uprising. Obviously the first was the more important so far as German interests were concerned. Nor should it be forgotten that in an age of imperialism the concern of Germany, then still itself an imperial power, for the rights of subject peoples can not have been more than limited. They would have had little principled sympathy for social and other "dissidents". They were experiencing in Poland in 1916 similar 'problems' to those the British were having in Ireland.

Other considerations were that a rising in Ireland might be expected to tie down British troops. If on sufficiently large a scale it might conceivably even draw British troops from the Western Front; it would certainly cause large-scale unrest and expense within the United Kingdom and it might even be possible to provide U-Boat stations along the Irish coast. (This prospect, translated into reality, became another MI6 propaganda assault that persisted into World War 2). Finally the German General Staff "reckoned on the possibility of a timely end to the war as the outcome of a successful uprising"[20].

---

[20] Spindler, Karl, *The Mystery of the Casement Ship,* Berlin, 1931 – originally an abridged edition, *Das Geheimenisvolle Schiff,* Berlin, 1920 - p. 265).

The Irish view remained that with Germany on the offensive and looking as if she could impose peace on her own terms, the timing for a rising was more opportune than it had ever been or was likely to be for years to come.

But the most important – and most overlooked – aspect of these negotiations from the Irish point of view was the undertaking from the German Government that if, by a rising, the Irish could establish their status as a nation deprived of lawful statehood, then Germany would afford them a hearing in that capacity at the post-war peace conference – expected to follow a German victory or favourable cease-fire.

Connolly's "Kidnapping"

The First World War changed the established tactics, strategy and philosophy of war in a way that not even the American Civil War had done. Napoleonic, all-decisive battle-victory was replaced by immense static lines of trench war, vast civilian involvement and mass destruction. But in 1914 the old concept still remained. A long drawn-out war of attrition, unconditional surrender and national humiliation on a vast scale was not foreseen. Even in 1916 such was still uncertain. In the summer of 1914 a war to 'be over by Christmas' with, perhaps, increased military influence and economic and territorial gains for one side and war reparations on a more or less acceptable scale from the other, as had been the case throughout the 19th century and earlier, was generally anticipated.

It was beyond belief that it would result in the destruction of empires, nations and cultures and would lead to a burgeoning belief (not to flower until post Hiroshima and Nagasaki thirty-one years later), in the capacity of great powers to destroy civilisation. Between 1914 and 1916 glimmerings of the unimaginable prospect of massive wars of attrition on a hitherto unknown scale nevertheless became mind-bogglingly evident. Accordingly, while German support for the Irish enterprise remained generally positive, enthusiasm began to wane as the war progressed.

Conditions for a successful rising were always governed by the deep secrecy of the IRB about their plans (which would give rise to confusion), and the effect that this and other evident military inadequacies had on their methodical military allies.

Casement's plan (calling for a German expeditionary force) was not an IRB plan. It is important to bear in mind that Casement was not a member of the IRB. But the IRB found him useful, primarily because of his connections with the German authorities.

For reasons usually – if not always – sound the professional military mind is notoriously wary of the amateur. Lives and sometimes great enterprises are at stake. Apparent inadequacies and uncertainties, even when allied to a *flaire* for improvisation, do not inspire confidence in the trained military mind at the best of times, let alone when battle is proposed.

However in any such considerations it is important to avoid straying into the notional minefield of thinking in terms of an IRB plan involving military victory. That was never an issue.

It is equally important to grasp the fact that The Rising achieved two of its primary objectives: - that is to say the Irish Republic was declared and broadcast to the world and separatist national fervour was aroused throughout the country. Within a short time a nationwide guerrilla war against British occupying forces, supported by the population in general and with the object of national self determination, was successfully undertaken in the name of the Republic declared in 1916 .

Of the three Irish objectives the only one not achieved was a place at the post war peace conference, and that was entirely outside Irish control.

Eoin MacNeill, Chief-of-Staff of the Volunteers, was *not* in the confidence of the IRB and did not know of plans for a rising. Supported by some senior Volunteer officers he favoured a strategy of reserving the Volunteers as a disciplined, but essentially protective, fighting force that would not act unless provoked. They were to be prepared for hostilities in the event of certain things happening – for instance an attempt to impose conscription or to disarm, arrest or detain the Volunteers and Volunteer leadership, in which event they were to resort to guerrilla warfare[21].

The small Citizen Army was more openly rebellious than were the Volunteers or the IRB. Throughout 1915, in his paper – *Irish Worker* - Connolly became increasingly belligerent, taunting the Volunteers to take action. He also wrote that if the German army landed in Ireland men of the working class would be perfectly entitled to join it: "if by so doing we could rid this country once and for all from its connection with the Brigand Empire that drags us unwillingly into this war". Unaware of IRB plans it seemed that Connolly was trying to "shame" the Volunteers into action.

Consequently – cautious as ever – they first arranged a meeting between Connolly, MacNeill and Pearse at which MacNeill urged Connolly to be cautious. But Connolly continued to press for an immediate insurrection, repeating his by then well-worn theme that whether or not the Volunteers came out, the Citizen Army would fight in Dublin.

"I said", MacNeill recalled some months later, "that if he counted in that event on compelling us to fight rather than

---

[21] As later events proved MacNeill's concept of guerrilla war was, in the circumstances and in practical military terms, a realistic view of the optimum strategy for a sustained campaign – provided the necessary conditions then existed, which they did not. A sustained campaign was not the intention of the IRB planners. In the event MacNeill's calamitous prevarication significantly weakened the military effectiveness of the Rising.

stand by and see his men destroyed, he was mistaken. We came to no agreement"[22].

Indeed not and Connolly continued to taunt the Volunteers in the *Irish Worker*. But in so doing he was putting at increasing risk the IRB's own plans for a rising that was intended to coincide with the upcoming German putsch – a subject of equal, if not greater, secrecy.

Padraic Pearse had been a member of the IRB since July, 1913. He was also a member of the Military Council and was Volunteer Director of Organization. He thus exercised considerable control over the Volunteers – probably, at that stage, even more than MacNeill himself.

The final meeting of the IRB Supreme Council before The Rising took place in January, 1916 [23]. It also coincided with an event that was to prove of the utmost significance.

By that stage Connolly's taunting was so serious a threat to IRB plans that they feared it might arouse the unwelcome attention of the British authorities (as was indeed the case, though it was insufficiently regarded by them). Pearse decided that the situation was so potentially damaging that some action was required as a matter of urgency. He arranged another meeting between MacNeill and Connolly; to no avail. Connolly was adamant that a Rising would take place soon, with or without the Volunteers. In retrospect it seems probable that the meeting would have been unfruitful anyway.

Neither Connolly nor MacNeill knew at that time of IRB plans for a rising. But then, suddenly and mysteriously Connolly disappeared on 19 January, to reappear just as suddenly and mysteriously three days later. From then on all critical references to the Volunteers vanished from the

---

[22] Lyons, op.cit., p.346, citing *Eoin MacNeill on the* 1914 *(sic.) Rising,* ed. F.X.Martin, IHS, xii, 246, Memorandum 11.

[23] It might be noted that this was five months before The Rising , also a strong indication of how far in advance the plans were made.

columns of his paper. What had happened to bring about this change during those three unaccounted for days?

Regarding details there are conflicting opinions. Some take the melodramatic view that Connolly was kidnapped by the IRB and held prisoner during which time he was somehow or another 'convinced' to lay-off, being released only just before his second-in-command, Michael Mallin, was about to confront the Volunteer Executive – which, of course, would have been pointless if Connolly was taken by the IRB.

But Connolly had the habit of disappearing unannounced if not, perhaps, for so long. By and large such a disappearance, even at a critical time when he was planning a rising himself, should not have been a cause for undue alarm by Mallin, as his brother subsequently confirmed was the case[24]. Connolly himself never spoke or wrote of his disappearance in any detail.

Others argue, equally improbably, that Connolly was captured, brought before the Military Council and told he'd be held prisoner unless he agreed not to take action before they were ready; that he held out for three days, finally agreeing to await the Council's decision, which resulted in the Military Council fixing Easter Sunday as the date for The Rising. It can be seen at once that such improvised and impractical behaviour from (hitherto) careful plotters who had spent eighteen months drawing up their plans, and three years honing the Volunteers to their purpose, makes little sense. The reality is simpler, credible and direct.

The general IRB plan already existed. There was, therefore, no need to hold Connolly for three days on that score. If we take the later accounts of Liam Mellows, Cathal Brugha and Nora Connolly O'Brien (Connolly's daughter), it becomes clear that Connolly was brought to a meeting with the Military Council – and there may well have been some element of persuasion initially involved in this. It is also clear

---

[24] Private conversation with the author.

that Connolly and the Council came to terms on a rising and that most of the three days was spent revising and fine-honing the plan. Additional confirmation, if needed, lies in the fact that Connolly was soon afterwards sworn into the IRB [25].

Rumours

On the British side things continued to be disorganised and confused. In November, two months earlier, Sir Mathew Nathan and Augustine Birrell, respectively Permanent Under-Secretary to the Lord Lieutenant (Wimborne) and Chief Secretary of Ireland, met two leading Unionists, Lord Midleton and Mr. Evelyn Cecil. Nathan confided to them that he believed Ireland was going downhill. Sinn Fein was elbowing aside Redmond and the IPP, the Volunteers were doing much mischief and 'the young priests' who supported them were very extreme[26]. But nothing much seems to have been done to bring the situation under control except, as we shall see, on paper.

In March (1916) Sir John French, GOC British Home forces (sacked, one recalls after the Curragh Mutiny) summarised reports on Ireland for the adjutant general RIC: - "Certain parts of Ireland are in a very disturbed state and

---

[25] In an Appendix (p. 268) to the second (1949) edition of his book, Desmond Ryan has this to say about Connolly's alleged kidnapping: "Joseph Plunkett told his sister, Mrs. Gertrude Dillon, in January, 1916, that Connolly had been decoyed into a taxi and driven to a house outside Dublin. Plunkett, Pearse, MacDermott were also in the car. They informed Connolly at once of their plans for insurrection....The discussions lasted three nights and the Rising plans, based on Plunkett's scheme, were adopted in outline. Connolly, at first angry, became so enthusiastic that his captors *could hardly persuade him to leave.*" The house was near Chapelizod.

[26] Leon 0 Broin, *Dublin Castle and the 1916 Rising*, p.54/55.

insurrection has been openly suggested in the public press –"
(a reference to Connolly's *Irish Worker*). Nevertheless he
turned down an offer of additional troops for Ireland.

On 22 March, Major Gen. G.M.W. MacDonagh, Director
of British Military Intelligence, told French that he had
received information from an absolutely reliable source that a
rising in Ireland was contemplated at an early date, and that
the Irish extremists were in communication with Germany.

A little later, just two weeks before The Rising,
information was given to Brigadier William Francis Howard
Stafford, British GOC Southern command at Queenstown
(Cobh), of plans for a German arms-landing in Kerry on 22
April. The information came from Admiral Sir Lewis Bayly,
also based in Queenstown, who was informed by Captain H.
C. Hall, head of British naval intelligence[27]. But, as late as 10
April, Nathan informed the Adjutant General that he did not
believe that the Sinn Fein leaders meant insurrection or, even
if the leaders did intend one, that he did not believe the
Volunteers had sufficient arms for the purpose (accurate
enough in one sense).

On that same day Major I. H. Price, Inspector-General of
the RIC and Irish Command intelligence officer, also
connected with the fledgling MI6, (who was to attend a
critical meeting in Dublin Castle on Easter Monday morning,
April 24th), informed Nathan that "There was undoubted
proof that Sinn Fein Irish Volunteers were working up for a
rebellion and revolution".

Nevertheless the IRB policy of secrecy was so effective
that right up to Spy Wednesday, a few days before The
Rising, the extraordinary fact is that not more than a handful
of men, including Casement (who, although not a member of
the IRB, was safely in Germany seeking help) and Devoy,
knew that a rising was intended – though not the details. That
fact that also seems to have helped give rise to the erroneous

---

[27] Notorious as the man who made use of the so-called "Black
Diaries" against Casement. He was also one of the prime movers
in the formation of MI6.

idea that The Rising was intended to be an all-out war against the British with possible victory as the impossible objective. Casement had sought a German expeditionary force of 50,000 men plus support, requiring major organisation, method and planning, in particular with regard to elementary logistics. Until the day of the Rising itself only the Military Council and three or four other Volunteer officers knew the operational plans. While this level of secrecy admirably protected the plan from betrayal, it also gave rise to confusion, particularly when there were orders and countermanding orders. That was a principal reason the Rising was not more widespread.

In January 1916 Asquith, the British prime-minister (if not for long) had indicated that compulsory conscription would be introduced. The announcement led to a major wave of anti-government feeling not just in Ireland, but in Britain as well. Later, together with the executions of the Irish leaders after The Rising, as well as the imposition of martial law, conscription became a major factor helping to swing public opinion in Ireland towards support of Sinn Fein.

Redmond, now far removed from the mood and feeling of the people, again dramatically wrong-footed himself. In spite of the virtual universal public opposition to conscription in Ireland, he publicly supported it! By then The Rising was just a week away.

The theology of rebellion in connection with the Rising has been strenuously argued, also often with prolific hindsight. "Men have wrestled with the problem of formulating a justification for the Easter Rising, but have not found it an easy task".[28] It is doubtful if the IRB members and others who planned and took part in it would agree. Justification for them was self-evident and inherited. Action was a matter of means and opportunity. It is clear that if the Rising had not taken place when it did, it would certainly

---

[28] F. X. Martin, 1916 – Revolution or Evolution, Leaders and Men, p.248.

have taken place soon afterwards. The reality appears to be, even by the standard of a 'just war', that the moral validity of the struggle of 1916 is almost unassailable. The Volunteers took and held the moral high ground, forcing the British into the invidious position that no matter what they did (and some of it was appalling) it could only reflect badly on themselves and force them – as had been the case on and off since 1798 - into contravening essential basic human rights and principles and, eventually, to war-crimes. Unarguably The Rising reawakened in the people an awareness, which had been eroded, of separate Irish identity.

Plans

Far from offering, or intending to offer, any prospect of military victory, the plans for the Rising outlined a strategy that envisaged a nationwide uprising concentrated initially on Dublin where the republic would be proclaimed while, with the arms and munitions from the German arms ship, wide-reaching preparatory dispositions took place elsewhere by Volunteers lightly, but well armed. After pre-planned action in Dublin, an orderly withdrawal westward to the line of the River Shannon (probably on the stretch Athlone/Portumna, Limerick/Killaloe), and guerrilla war before surrender, would follow. The intention was that this would revitalise the people – as it did – and attract international attention to the fact that the will of the Irish people was for independence, thus creating the circumstances necessary for Ireland to be recognised at the post-war peace conference as a belligerent nation.

The argument is also heard that it was all a lost cause since Germany lost the war. But that happened in 1918. In 1916 Germany and the other Central Powers looked like winning the war, or at least certainly forcing an advantageous peace. America had not entered the war on the side of the Allies and showed no intention of doing so on either side.

92

Irish strategy, therefore, was not as doom-laden as is sometimes postulated by misdated arguments. True, the dynamic and extent of the grand design of the plan went sadly awry at the critical moment, in particular the failure of the landing of arms in Tralee Bay by the arms ship *Aud*. But the question is – were the purpose and outcome affected?

A common misconception is that these arms were meant for Dublin. Again it takes but a moment to appreciate that if this were so they could hardly have been landed in a more awkward place. But the arms were not destined for Dublin. They were to arm the Volunteers of the south and west and enable them to take and hold the proposed Shannon line until the rendezvous with the Dublin Volunteers, expected to total 2,000 – 2,500.

What went wrong? We come to the sad and difficult questions concerning Eoin MacNeill and his countermanding order that would throw the entire Rising into confusion. MacNeill felt that not only he himself, Chairman of the Volunteer overall Committee, but the entire Volunteer organisation, had been deceived by the "war-party". And so they had. But not only were the Volunteers the only body capable of making a rising possible, they had, as we know, been created by the IRB in 1913 - deviously it is true - for that precise purpose. By 1916 ordinary Volunteers were well aware of this purpose – even if not of the plan or timing. To argue that a majority of them did not anticipate a rising at some stage or another is unrealistic.

From late 1915 and through the winter and spring of 1916 MacNeill seems to have suspected that there was a plan but, apart from seeking assurances from Pearse - which he received - he does not appear to have taken any steps to verify any such suspicions.

Then, on 19 April, Spy Wednesday, a mysterious paper known as 'The Castle Document', apparently signed by General Friend, British GOC, Dublin, enters the picture. In brief it was an order for the widespread and immediate arrest of members "of all national organisations, for the military occupation of certain premises and the isolation of others (including the house of the Archbishop of Dublin)", involving large-scale raids on the entire Volunteer leadership throughout the country[29]. Some claim that this document was a forgery by Plunkett and/or MacDonagh intended to provoke the Volunteers (particularly MacNeill) into action. Others, in view of confirmed plans by Dublin Castle authorities to round up 'Sinn Fein' leaders, hold that it was genuine.

While its provenance has never been verified there is no reason to suppose it wasn't both. It is altogether inconceivable to suppose that the military authorities did not have a contingency plan to round up and arrest Volunteer and Sinn Fein leaders – which, in fact, they did and, as we shall see, were about to put it into execution.

The plan, advocated by Lt. Col. W. Edgeworth at the vice-regal lodge on Easter Sunday (23 April), followed the broad outline of the 'Castle Document'. Moreover it is not unlikely that Plunkett, having seen or obtained details of the genuine article, may well have 'modified' it to suit IRB intentions.

On Spy Wednesday, too, Alderman Tom Kelly read this document to Dublin Corporation when it was described as a decipher of a paper on the official files of the Castle. That it was genuine and that it may also have been used in order to provoke MacNeill and the Volunteers to compliance with IRB, are far from being mutually exclusive[30]. It was alleged by Patrick J. Little, the editor of *New Ireland*, that it was intended by the British to provoke armed resistance.

Understandably, if unbelievably, the British officially denied that any such document existed, or ever had existed.

But on learning of it MacNeill issued a general order to the Volunteers to resist suppression – itself, as we have noted, a guarantee of armed conflict.

---

[29] See Dorothy Macardle, *The Irish Republic*, pps 158 et seq.

[30] MacNeill's position was that the Volunteers would resist any attempt by the British to disarm or arrest them.

Whether the document was a *ruse de guerre* by Plunkett and MacDonagh or a genuine Castle plan there can be no doubt whatever that the British must have had written contingency plans for the arrest of the Irish leaders. To think otherwise is to attribute to them a truly mind-boggling level of incompetence.

It was on Holy Thursday night that Bulmer Hobson learned from J.J. (Ginger) O'Connell that general command orders had been issued for a Rising on Easter Sunday. He immediately informed MacNeill who went with Hobson and O'Connell to confront Pearse.

MacNeill declared that he would do everything possible - 'short of informing the government' - to stop the insurrection. Pearse answered that MacNeill was powerless to do so, adding – with presentiment, but to no avail - that interference now would only cause confusion. MacNeill left to prepare orders countermanding those issued by Pearse for Sunday. However, before issuing these orders on Good Friday, Pearse, McDonagh and MacDermott persuaded him that to do so would not only be counter-productive, but also extremely dangerous. To do so would, they argued (correctly as it turned out), create confusion, would be ignored in many areas and while they would not prevent a rising, such orders would significantly weaken it. MacNeill remained unmoved until he learned of the German arms shipment. He then agreed to allow the mobilisation orders stand. He went further and drafted a general warning, intended to bring the Volunteers to readiness, that government action to suppress the Volunteers was inevitable and might begin at any moment.

But by then the vital arms shipment had gone completely awry.

The Arms Ship

The story of the arms ship, *Aud*, is like a tale from Joseph Conrad that includes high drama, wartime secrecy and great adventure coupled with a last minute unseen and unheralded backlash of Fate that rose like a dripping Triton from the threshing sea between the Blasket Islands, the last outpost of Europe facing the mighty Atlantic, and the mainland at Dunquin and Dun an Oir, where the Spanish had sent forces in support of the Irish against the Tudor conquistadors some 300 years earlier.

The story is recounted by Karl Spindler, Leutnant, Kaiserlich Kriegsmarine and Captain of the ship[31]. From the time that Casement first went to Germany in 1914 German/Irish consultations on plans for a rising had been continuous. By late 1915 the Central Powers - Germany, Austro-Hungary, Turkey – confidently anticipated a satisfactory peace settlement. It was also, however, a time when the German High Command would have been cautious about diverting military resources from the Western Front and what was intended to be the decisive battle at Verdun. France, not the relatively small British Expeditionary Force, was Germany's principal and most dangerous adversary. Consequently Casement's initial request for 50,000 troops with naval, air and artillery support fell on deaf ears.

For reasons that may now seem obscure and unrealistic Casement looms much larger in British views of The Rising than was merited. But the reason is not really hard to find. Casement – 'Sir Roger' in the British social register (though he refused and returned the honour) - was a notable member of the British Establishment who had revealed to the world the appalling conditions of slave labour in both the Congo and in Putamayo in South America. He was, if not quite an aristocrat, at least a leader and representative of all good things British. Here was a man unquestionably of distinction and proven capacity, an adornment of all that imperial thoroughbred status was supposed to be. And what, incredibly, did he do? He betrayed that great trust! He

---

[31] See *The Mystery of the Casement Ship,* Berlin, 1931 – *Das Geheimnisvolle Schiff*, Berlin, 1920. Also *The Sea and the Easter Rising,* John de Courcy Ireland.

disavowed all that he represented, was heir to, and had been honoured with, and had gone to the dogs of Irish republicanism. Even worse, he supported and deserted to the German enemy, taking with him all his accumulated knowledge and leadership expertise.

Before he went to Germany from New York, in September, 1914, Casement wrote an open letter to the Press (following the disclosure that Home Rule for Ireland would not come into operation and was to be further amended), in which he castigated British rule there and, as Connolly was to do, advised Irishmen to join the German forces if they set foot in Ireland.

This must certainly have moved Casement to the top of the British "Black List" - a by no means mythical catalogue – and was almost certainly what roused the hostility of the British Establishment so powerfully against him and conferred on him a role and responsibility about The Rising that was completely exaggerated. There is no doubt that Casement, hanged for treason where the other executed leaders were shot, was subjected to a ferocious campaign of vilification both during his trial and after.

What is also noteworthy in considering the overall scheme of things is that the plan to send arms to Ireland was made some six months before The Rising. However it is at this point that the sequence of events began that were – albeit inadvertently and, astonishingly, without affecting the outcome – to dislocate utterly the IRB's plan. Unexpectedly, as well as the German and Irish planners, several non-IRB people are said to have known of the plan. But that remains doubtful[32].

The particular catastrophe so far as the vital arms were concerned is that just before *Aud* sailed alterations to the date and place of the proposed landing different to those Spindler had been instructed to observe were made in broadcast

---

[32] Spindler, op. cit., p.238.

transmissions between Ireland, New York and Berlin[33]. A raid by the American secret service on the German mission in New York brought the transcripts to light. One included the specific demand that the arms landing should not take place until the night of Easter Sunday, 23 April. The Americans passed this information to the British.

In addition the British had broken German codes and were monitoring all wireless traffic to and from Germany. They picked up messages between John Devoy in New York and Berlin. British naval and military authorities in Ireland were alerted.

The British, accordingly, learned that 20,000 rifles, ten machine guns and 4,000,000 rounds of ammunition, as well as 400 kilograms of explosives, were to be landed at Tralee Bay 'between April 20th and April 23rd'. The dates, however, were wrong, moving the timetable by as much as three days - a flaw that was to have disastrous consequences.

The arms were loaded aboard the captured English steamer *Castro,* renamed *Libau,* which sailed from Lübeck on Sunday, 9 April. While *Libau* was a very suitable modern steamer, it did not have wireless.

Booby-trapped and disguised as the Norwegian trader *Aud,* with the words AUD- NORGE painted in large letters on its sides, *Libau* carried a cargo of pit-props, tin baths, enamelled steel-ware, wooden doors, window-frames and other building materials besides the hidden main cargo. After a voyage that took her above the Arctic Circle, Spindler successfully made landfall in accordance with his instructions on the afternoon of Friday, 21 April – three days too early! For those three days he lay between Inishtooshkert and the mainland waiting for a pilot to bring him to Fenit pier. No one came. What had happened?

---

[33] 'Irish leader Devoy tells me that revolution begins Ireland Easter Sunday stop Request deliver arms between Good Friday and Easter Sunday   Limerick Westcoast Ireland stop protracted waiting impossible comma desire cabled answer whether may promise help from Germany - Bernstorff', (Imperial German Embassy, New York, telegram No. 675).

The Irish did not expect the arms ship before Sunday, as planned. But, because of the message from Devoy, the Germans believed that they were expected any time between Thursday and Sunday.

The British were better informed, but all but failed to convert the information into intelligence. As well as the information already received through their own intelligence services the information gained through the raid of the American Secret Service on the German Legation in New York was available to them. But *Aud* had sailed by the time corrected messages were made and did not have wireless, so confirmation of the date did not reach her.

In the Blasket sound the signal for *Aud* from the Irish was two green fishing lamps to be shown between Easter Saturday evening and the early hours of Easter Monday. Vice-Commandant Patrick Cahill of the Tralee battalion, the local Volunteer commander, was ready with these for the appropriate dates.

Ironically when, following her horrendous journey, *Aud* steamed precisely between the Blaskets and the mainland on Friday 21st April, Spindler, congratulated himself on his precise timing, and looked in vain for the signal from the mainland. And there would be another ironic twist of fate. That very day, as the pilot, Mort O'Leary of Castlegregory was on his way home after meeting Cahill, he spotted *Aud* lying off Inishtooshkert, but had no reason to think it was the ship with the precious arms he was waiting for[34].

The story of Casement and the landing is just as dramatic, romantic and tragic. As we know while Casement was aware of plans for a rising, he was not in the IRB or privy to the details of its plans and its set purpose. Clearly refusal of the Germans to provide the invasion force he sought led him to

---

[34] He being told that the German ship would be a small one and that she would not arrive before Easter Sunday at the earliest, so he presumed that she was a British ship.' (Max Caulfield, *The Easter Rebellion,* p.49).

conclude that hope of a military victory was out of the question and that a rising should be postponed[35].

This has also helped give rise to the equally false assumption (also a likely British propaganda item) commonly stated by some historians in spite of all the evidence to the contrary, that he came to Ireland with the intention of 'stopping' the Rising.

Even if it were within his power to have done so nothing in Casement's writings supports this view. While he was certainly opposed to a rising at that time, it was not the case that he returned to do 'his best to' try to stop it. He returned in order to take part. It is also possible that the theory that he came to stop the Rising originated with Eva Gore-Booth (Countess Markievicz's sister), who, during Casement's trial, made precisely this allegation - presumably trying to mitigate the case against him[36].

And, of course, he never had the power or authority, attributed to him by the British, of being in a position to "stop" the rising. To conclude otherwise contradicts the obvious.

Captain Robert Monteith, Casement's lieutenant who accompanied him and landed with him at Banna strand in Kerry, categorically denies the allegation[37].

Leaving aside the reference to "sanctioning", which was never within his power, the final words on the matter must

---

[35] His conclusions may well have contributed to the ludicrous and erroneous idea of military victory over the British being part of the IRB plan.

[36] See extract from Sir Basil Thompson's diaries for 22 July, 1916, cited by Alfred Noyes *The Accusing Ghost or Justice for Casement,* London, 1957, p. 17.

[37] He wrote: "Another error into which some writers have fallen is the assumption that Casement tried to stop the. Rising. This is not even a half-truth", (Robert Monteith *Casements Last Adventure).* Mackey also deals peremptorily with these falsehoods.

surely be those of the man himself whose prison manuscript includes the following: "I want to make it very plain that I approve of the Rising – failure and all – in one sense. As a man of 'travelled mind and understanding' I should never have sanctioned[38] it had I been in Ireland, but since those there were bent on it, I, too (like the O'Rahilly) would have gone with it".

Interestingly and in spite of his involvement in the United States and Germany, and that The Rising was about to take place, Casement remained under the impression that it was a Volunteer, not an IRB plan, a view which was evidently encouraged by both Plunketts when they met him in Germany.

When Casement arrived in Ireland by U-boat he was extremely ill. Soon after coming ashore he was discovered and was arrested.

Preparations and Confusion

Spindler's orders were to wait for half an hour 'and if no pilot boat with a green flag at the masthead and a man with a green jersey in the bows is at the rendezvous, and there does not appear to be any possibility of communicating with them, you are to use your own judgement as to whether to proceed or turn back'. All Thursday and throughout the night until Good Friday he waited in the narrows between the Blaskets and the mainland, when his luck finally ran out. After two burlesque encounters with the British navy *Aud* was escorted to Cork harbour on Good Friday, where Spindler successfully scuppered his ship and its cargo, together with the IRB hope of arms from Germany.

When MacNeill received the fatal news about *Aud* he contacted Pearse to get him to call the rising off. Pearse

---

[38] Casement's use of the word "sanctioned", apart from its being written under great stress, would anyway be intended to convey "joined in formal agreement or confirmation" at that time.

refused. His final assertion is definitive: '...I am satisfied that we should have accomplished the task of enthroning, as well as proclaiming, the Irish Republic as a Sovereign State had our arrangements for a simultaneous rising of the whole country, with a combined plan as sound as the Dublin plan has proved to be, been allowed to go through on Easter Sunday...' [39].

MacNeill, however, sent Volunteer officers through the country with the message:- "Volunteers completely deceived. All orders for special action are hereby cancelled, and on no account will action be taken". He also published a countermanding notice in the *Sunday Independent.*

Nevertheless the Military Council decided to proceed on Easter Monday and on Easter Sunday night another order went out from the Military Council to all Volunteer battalion commands in Dublin:

GENERAL HEADQUARTERS,
April 24. *1916.*
The four city battalions will parade for inspection and route march at 10 a.m. to-day. Commandants will arrange centres. Full arms and equipment, and one day's rations.
Thomas MacDonagh,
Commandant.

Summary: Excluding the aborted one of Connolly and the Citizen Army we can therefore see that there were three plans for a potential rising. These were-
1. Casement's attempt to get a large German expeditionary force to land in Ireland;
2. the reactive plan of the Volunteers to rise in the event of certain hostile actions being taken by the British, and

---

[39] *Manifesto, Collected Works*, P.H.Pearse. The use of the word 'enthroning' is interesting and can only refer to the anticipated peace conference.

102

3. the IRB plan that came to fruition.

It may also be readily seen how, over time, the three may have been combined by some writers, with additional confusion.

The question is:- Why did the hard headed men who had so patiently and carefully planned for a nation-wide rising go ahead in Dublin following MacNeill's countermanding order, the loss of the Aud and a 24-hour postponement, when all prospect of arms or troops from Germany was gone, when any possibility of the rest of the country rising as well was less than probable and in the almost certain knowledge that less than one third the force needed to seize and hold the strategic positions in Dublin was available?

There is but one real answer.

It is that the time was opportune and might not soon come again. It is probable – whatever about arguments such as that The Rising would have taken place sooner or later – that the leaders' perception was that unless they acted and unless The Rising took place and lasted for at least three days the German undertaking to grant Ireland belligerent nation status and a hearing at the post-war peace conference in order to reaffirm the nation and its independence would evaporate and be swallowed up in the smoke and thunder of a war in Europe that had little or no bearing on Irish aspirations.

In addition there was the powerful flood-tide of combined republican dedication and the crusading spirit of social justice that had taken hold of the Irish workers and stirred them to rebellious anger. None of this is a likely basis for a sudden explosion of romantic "blood-sacrifice", which, nevertheless, is what, for decades, The Rising is held to have been. It should now be clear that this prejudicial description is no more than British propaganda, as also is the fact that the fiction was maintained until it all but overwhelmed the reality.

Beyond all reasonable expectation The Rising achieved two of its three important objectives. The Irish Republic had been proclaimed to the world. In compliance with von Clausewicz's third aim of war, separatist national fervour was so successfully

103

reawakened in Ireland that within two years the people, in the name of the Republic, overwhelmingly supported both the separatist movement at the polls and a nationwide guerrilla war against British occupation. This extraordinary and unexpected achievement of the 'Shinners' had to be countered and dismissed as fully as possible. Nothing but effective counter-propaganda could achieve that and, with confidence, determination and startling effect and success, the fledgling MI6 stepped into this breach [40].

As already noted only the third objective of the IRB plan would be denied the Irish, and that by circumstances unforeseen and unlikely from the perspective of 1916 – namely an Allied victory in 1918 gained finally with US help.

In terms of overall population (about five million people) the Ireland of 1916 was not dissimilar to that of the early 2000s. But demographically (as in other matters), it was a very different place. Dublin - and other principal cities - were between one-third and one-fourth their present size. Most of the population lived in the country and rural values were stronger and exercised far more influence on life in general. The land agitation of the previous forty years had left in the rural heart of Ireland not alone a powerful feeling for justice and independence, but also an alert awareness of infringements of perceived social and human rights. In addition to the urban rebelliousness typified by the Dublin Strike of 1913, that situation provided fertile ground for the IRB.

---

[40] The author has considerable professional experience in dealing with information/national propaganda. Then Director of the Government Information Bureau he organised, controlled and directed the Irish Government international information and publicity campaign 1969/1973, countering and challenging the world-wide propaganda of the British and Northern Ireland Office in relation to the dreadful events which, from the summer of 1969 afflicted Northern Ireland. It was the first such major internationally focussed government campaign since the foundation of the State and it successfully achieved its objectives.

104

On the threshold of war in 1914 the British Government concluded that they faced what they were pleased to call 'an unexpected Irish problem', although this had for years been moving towards inevitability. Already taking shape was the perceptible shift in political thinking by a populace familiar with the revolutionary spirit of the nineteenth century and a background of sustained justification going back to the Rising of 1798, from (failed) constitutional methods towards independence.

"The military objective of The Rising was to seize and hold Dublin City; to hold it openly as the army of the Irish people; to hold it in such a manner that the British would be forced to attack; on such a scale that that it would be obvious that the capital city, and not a few back streets, were held; and for sufficient length of time to ensure it could not be written off as just a riot or a street brawl ...the occupation of the city had a strategic as well as a tactical significance. A battle for its possession had a strategic as well as a tactical aim"[41].

In spite of the warnings received, the Dublin Castle authorities did not anticipate significant trouble from 'the Sinn Feiners'[42].

What reason was there for such complacency in wartime? It seems that, like Redmond – on whose advice the authorities in Dublin Castle presumably placed reliance – they were so out of touch with the country, and so ingrained was the idea of their being in a mere temporary capacity until Redmond and a Home Rule government took over in due

---

[41] Col. Eoghan O Neill, *The Battle of Dublin* 1916, *An Cosantoir,* May, 1966, p. 215.

[42] On April 10th, the very day he reported to Nathan that there was 'undoubted proof' that Sinn Fein and the Irish Volunteers were working up for a rebellion and revolution', Major Price, also submitted a memorandum stating: 'The general state of Ireland, apart from recruiting and apart from the activities of the pro-German Sinn Fein minority, is thoroughly satisfactory'.

course, that they adopted an attitude of thoughtlessly letting well enough alone.

But, however placatory or indifferent the administration's attitude may have been towards republicanism, there was a major flaw to such logic. It did not follow that republicanism would not take the offensive against the British.

The Arguments

A fundamental issue that did give rise to considerable confusion during the Rising, and interpretation of which is still very confused today, concerns the formation and intent of the Irish Volunteers. They were founded in 1913 following the establishment of the Ulster Volunteer Force.

But it was by no means a simple question of counteraction. Forming the Volunteers was an IRB plan. The IRB had already (in 1873) created in secret a potential provisional republican government and president. Now they took the opportunity to promote the formation of the Volunteers as a prospective fighting force of theirs – but that fact was kept a strict secret, particularly from the Volunteer leadership, of which Professor Eoin MacNeill was chief-of-staff

As a result the Volunteers were to come under not one, but two, military command structures, one of which did not know of the existence of the other.

Accordingly there were very different ideas – and plans – as to how the Volunteers might take the field in the event of a Rising.

So far as the Volunteer leadership was concerned the troops, in certain circumstances – i.e. if an attempt was made to arrest or disarm them, or if conscription were introduced, would resort to guerrilla warfare against the enemy and continue as long as possible.

The IRB plans were very different. Even many senior officers of the Volunteers who were also members of the IRB knew little of the Rising plan. The planners were members of a small military council or committee, established and charged in 1914, with drawing up the plan in secret.

The Rising claimed the freedoms it set out to achieve in the only manner possible in the climate of time when both religion and social morality were endemic[43].

In order to clarify things more effectively it is worth summarising some of what we have already considered, namely the climate of the times in which the Rising occurred.

1. Although already crumbling, capitalistic, exploitative imperialism was the worldwide dominating political and economic force.

2. The crumbling was partly the result of social change driven by a variety of socialist doctrines, in the main promoting the cause and interests of human rights, if not always precisely in those terms.

3. The exhaustive War itself had been thrust upon the helpless masses of the world by the power-blind and system-bound imperial war-lords of France, Germany, Britain, Austro-Hungary, Russia and the Ottoman Empire set on a course of supremacy that was in fact one of all-round virtual self-destruction.

4. The pan-European socialist movement that had lifted the appalling plight of the worker and his family from despair to aspiration eventually reached this colonised western outpost and, in the hands of people like James Larkin, James Connolly and Madame Markiewicz, led to the great assertion of rights that was the 1913 strike.

5. Circumstances ordained that this movement for social justice coincided to a large extent with two other developments having an important bearing

---

[43] It seems lamentable that today the country has moved from being a proud and dignified nation to a mere economy. As one writer put it: "we have become the epitome of the cultureless, soulless state".(Jim Sullivan, Rathedmond, Sligo, Irish Times (28.0.'06)

on the Rising. The first of these was the Irish cultural movement that, between about 1890 and 1916, laid firm hold on popular outlook and imagination and generated a powerful wave of interest and activity in the GAA, the Gaelic League, The Abbey Theatre, Feiseanna and many other examples, the significance and influence of which movements – with the exception of the GAA – is easily overlooked today. The second was, of course, the rise and development of aligned armed forces in the country. The Ulster Volunteer Force was established primarily to oppose Home Rule and as the sectarian army of the treasonable Provisional Government of Ulster set up by Carson and his cohorts when they proposed to establish such a statelet in 1914, just before the outbreak of the war. It was, with impeccable irony, to have been established under the aegis of the German Kaiser. The Irish Volunteers – not tolerated by the British authorities as they tolerated the UVF – and the Citizen Army were established, principally in the south, as an apparent counter-force – the first, as we have seen, in reality as an IRB force.

6. Into this uneasy and unstable situation there erupted two very provocative events. The first of these was the treasonable refusal of elements of the officer corps of the British Army stationed at the Curragh – cavalry – to act to prevent hostile action by the UVF. This extraordinary incident is often overlooked by commentators who wish to minimise what was a seriously treasonable action (the first by the British Army since their civil war). Not so well known is the fact that a substantial majority of these officers came from the landed Irish Protestant class with identical backgrounds to those who ran the UVF. Like

Carson's treasonable provisional government the incident was swept under the carpet of British interests on the outbreak of war.

The other was the massacre by British troops of unarmed civilians at Bachelor's Walk in Dublin shortly afterwards. That appalling event stirred the public heart as perhaps nothing up to then had done, and the ranks of the recently formed Irish Volunteers were multiplied by new recruits.

However that particular gain was short-lived when John   Redmond, would-be leader of a Home Rule party in an imaginary Irish administration, followed in the unsteady footsteps of those who brought about the Union yoke, and exhorted the Volunteers to fight for Britain for – believe it or not – the rights of small nations.

In the meantime, as we know, adhering to perhaps the strongest national influence of all that had been continuous since 1798, the IRB had other plans.

These are some of the things that contributed to the atmosphere of the year 1916 and influenced much of society at that time.

We can no longer, thank God, experience the appalling poverty, the rancid, foetid smells of the worst slums in Europe, the rank misery and despair of the people who lived – more or less survived – in them; sense their despair; see the bare-foot and vermin-infested children playing in the open gutters that were little more than sewers; above all have any idea of the barren hopelessness and struggle for mere survival that filled each and every day of these people's – perhaps mercifully – short lives.

Irish rural and other basic wages ranged between one third and one half of wages for equivalent work in England and between one half and two thirds of that in Wales and Scotland.

We can have no notion of the contempt with which the Irish worker was treated by the colonial lords and masters, from the Castle down to the lowest ranking clerk. But, unless we open our hearts and our minds to the reality that it was – much less, as so many try to do, condescendingly judge that time by some self-serving version of today's values – we have little or no hope of getting any kind of accurate view of how and why the people responded to the Rising with such overwhelming support immediately after the event, in a monumental justification of von Clausewitz's third rule of war, and pursued and enshrined its objectives, then held for more than a hundred years.

We know what the IRB plan for the Rising was – and that it had nothing to do with a stand-up battle with British forces. But, as we have also seen, there is some excuse for this erroneous view.

First cause of confusion.

Both the British – inasmuch as they considered the matter at all – and the head of the Irish Volunteers, Eoin MacNeill, did believe that any military confrontation must be along such "stand up and fight" lines. MacNeill envisaged country-wide guerrilla warfare.

Yet one of the most fascinating, and seldom heard facts in this context is that even if the Rising had not taken place when it did, and even in spite of MacNeill's countermanding order, a confrontation during that week was inevitable anyway.

Even as the Citizen Army attacked the gates of Dublin Castle on Easter Monday a meeting was taking place inside. It was attended by Sir Mathew Nathan, Permanent under-secretary, Arthur Hamilton Norway, Secretary of the post office and Major Ivan Price, Inspector-General of the RIC, chief intelligence officer of the British Army in Ireland. That meeting followed one the previous night with the Lord Lieutenant, Lord Wimborne, where it was decided to arrest,

110

and disarm Volunteers throughout the country and deport the leaders.

Any such attempt would have been the signal MacNeill was ready to accept for the Volunteers to resist in arms.

Moblisation.

As we know, because of MacNeill's countermanding order, less than one third of the anticipated Volunteer muster in Dublin mobilised. As a result many intended positions could not be occupied and those that were seriously undermanned and communications between them was negligible or haphazard – another serious source of confusion. Moreover for the same reason communications with the rest of the country were affected with the result that hard information and intelligence was scarce to the point of being non-existent and rumour became rife.

MacNeill

There is no doubt that MacNeill dithered between Friday and Saturday night. That uncertainty was translated into destructive action so far as the Rising was concerned when he learned of the capture of Casement and Aud. It must be remembered that even at that stage, so far as we know, MacNeill thought in terms of guerrilla military confrontation. In view of his actions it seems unlikely that he was aware of, or understood, the IRB/Military Committee objectives for the Rising. And so there was another cause of confusion.

Conflicting Orders

This applied in the main to rural areas, primarily because of lack of communication with Dublin.

Secrecy

With which the IRB/Military Committee had made their plans. Right up to the last moment only a handful of people on a need-to-know basis had any idea 1/ that the Rising was planned, 2/ what local dispositions and actions were to be. The reason for this intense secrecy was based on what was known of leaks in 1798 and 1803. However, the small turnout effectively limited whatever arrangements there may have been to coordinate the overall plan.

Finally, the chain of command.

Even if there had been a complete turn-out the chain-of-command structure does not seem to have been clear. Local commanders were, it appears – and for some of the reasons mentioned above – to be left largely to their own devices once the outbreak began, subject to the general overall plan. In fact this was probably unavoidable, but it certainly would have contributed to the general confusion. Pearse, as commander-in-chief, and Connolly as commander in Dublin, were not appointed to these posts until Monday morning. How significant that is open to question since both were involved in the planning for months past, such orders as they issued were accepted and the appointments may well have been simply regulatory.

From the outset, the IRB manipulated and honed the Volunteers as their instrument to be used at the opportune time, and did so without MacNeill, Chief-of-Staff of the Volunteers and other non-IRB members knowing of it[44].

---

[44] In their expert summaries Maj.General P.J. Halley (*The Irish Press*, April 9, 1966 and in *The Irish Sword*, Winter 1966, Summer 1967), and An Colonel Eoghan O Neill in a brilliant analysis (*An Cosantoir*, May, 1966), show that the military planning for the rising was excellent. In evidence before the Royal Commission held after the Rising Major Price, Irish Command Intelligence Officer for the British Army, said "There is no doubt that the outbreak had been planned very carefully ... the work of

Important differences between MacNeill and the IRB as to the kind of campaign the Irish might conduct in the event of war were also significant. Like Casement MacNeill wrote in terms of a guerrilla campaign and possible military victory – (perhaps a further reason for the notion that The Rising was based on this idea). But, as we know, MacNeill also insisted that the Volunteers should not act unless provoked.

On the other hand the IRB plan envisaged using the Volunteers and the Citizen Army as the strike force for insurrection, with additional help from Germany (See Appendix 1)[45]. It was not a question of if, but of when. By 1916 the officer ranks of the Volunteers were so infiltrated by the IRB that there was little doubt that the bulk of the Volunteers were by then more attuned to the drumbeat of the IRB than to that of the Volunteer leaders.

While one purpose of The Rising was a free republic, there was also the clear perception that it would not of itself achieve that objective. But it would be the means towards that end. As we know the intention was to declare Ireland's independence, to proclaim a republic and to obtain the hearing promised by Germany at the peace-conference.

---

organisation was very complete." The common error in thinking that the objective of The Rising was military victory needs to be closed. That was never the case. There were three complete copies of the plan. Today none survives. We must reconstruct. But it is not simple guesswork. There are several complementary first-hand accounts of the overall plan. The facts of the planning from 1914 and the action itself clarify much, as the author has shown in *Birth of a Republic* and as research and the informed studies of Nora Connolly O'Brien, Florence O'Donoghue, General Halley and Colonel O'Neill demonstrate.

[45] It is not only characteristic, but symptomatic, of most of the leaders of 1916 - and, indeed, of most of those who led the War of Independence - that they were motivated, and sometimes wracked, by profound moral considerations. Idealism had not then been displaced by material cynicism.

Unlike the idea of military victory in the field, that constitutional victory was realisable.

There are four customary arguments against the Rising. They are, firstly, that it shouldn't have taken place because Home Rule would bring all that was expected anyway (in a risible extension of this hopeless idea the curious point has even been made that The Rising was wrong because the values that inspired it are not those of today's so-called liberal ethic.)

As outlined in Part One this argument is at best an academic exercise. By 1914 Home Rule was a failed programme. Both the Irish Citizen Army and the IRB had determined on a rising before the end of the war; if the Rising had not taken place at Easter, 1916, it would certainly have occurred soon afterwards. In the event 1916 seemed the most propitious time.

Casement expressed it: ... "The case of Ireland is desperate; it is now or never. Ireland can wait less than any other country the world. If she is not helped now all the help of Christendom a few years hence cannot restore her as Ireland ... an Irish Party might very credibly be in existence 30 years hence ... attending just as regularly at Westminster – but there will be no Ireland"[46].

The second argument against the Rising is the one we are most familiar with – that it was a "blood-sacrifice" cobbled together by impractical, romantic idealists and poets. This argument has no merit, but used as a clever phrase suggesting mindless immolation, "blood sacrifice" is an excellent piece of "Black propaganda". The argument continues that the leaders were idealists, some of them even poets, who conceived this hopeless "blood-sacrifice", but couldn't make it succeed ("success" being the nonsensical notion that the leaders believed they could take on and beat the British Army in Ireland in the field).

---

[46] Mackey, pps. 17, 18.

114

To diminish and belittle one of the few genuinely idealistic and honourable world events of the period in such a way is contemptible and is as preposterous as the suggestion that poetry and military ability are mutually exclusive, in spite of all the evidence - from Xenophon onwards - to the contrary.

Major General P. J. Halley wrote: "There is a widely held opinion that the Rising ... was organised and led by impracticable intellectuals and dreamers who impulsively led their followers into an unplanned and impossible military situation which could only have one end, the destruction of those taking part ...[that they] were incapable of clear military planning ... I must disagree"[47].

Here we might ask if the following does not provide a basis for similar "reams of cant": *"The tree of liberty must continually be watered with the blood of martyrs and tyrants"*.

But it wasn't written by Pearse. It was written by Thomas Jefferson. Is it then to be argued that the American war of Independence was also no more than a pointless "blood-sacrifice"?

Among the executed leaders of The Rising those who were poets included Padraic Pearse, Thomas MacDonagh and Joseph Mary Plunkett -- three of the key IRB planners. It is part of their legacy that they helped make possible the freedom in which such mindless nonsense can be articulated and written. Curiously enough no such demeaning criticism has been levelled at the tough, pragmatic men and women, many of them survivors of 1916, who led the nation in war and peace thereafter. Do the Sir Oracles expounding such clap-trap therefore expect us to believe that all the poets and romantics were killed in 1916 and that none but the pragmatists survived?

---

[47] Desmond Greaves adds: "Reams of cant have been poured over a few rhetorical phrases of Pearse's such as 'There are many things more horrible than bloodshed, and slavery is one of them'", *1916 As History*.

115

It would be more to the point to consider in whose interests it is to diminish the Rising and its leaders and sneer at their motives and accomplishments.

"Blood Sacrifice", Cui Bono?

The most common false criticism of the Rising - the one most prevalent and sinister – is the "blood-sacrifice" label. It is certainly the oldest. It has been around a long time, coming into currency soon after the Rising itself. It is often attributed to Pearse. But whatever about his idealistic commitment to a noble sacrifice in a noble cause, there is no record of Pearse ever having said or written the phrase. So where does it come from?

The implication is clear; the Rising was a mad, romantic gesture; a pointless offering of innocent blood by a group of poets; a gesture that combined the mystical imagery of Easter and that of nationalists – and so on. What it is not is any kind of genuine definition of the Rising. What is the reason for that?

Cui bono? Who or what stood or stands to benefit from the Rising being so denigrated?

Pearse did write that:-"There are many things more horrible than bloodshed, and slavery is one of them". And it may be from that or something similar that the censorious "blood-sacrifice" label was coined.

Yet, to cite Thomas Jefferson again:- "The tree of liberty must be refreshed from time to time with the blood of patriots and martyrs." That is not only a similar phrase to that of Pearse's – the expression is much closer to a "blood sacrifice" idea. Is it the case, then, as asked above, that the American war of independence was also a romantic and pointless "blood sacrifice"?

There seems little doubt that "blood sacrifice" is too significant and too widespread a term to have arisen casually. It is hard to imagine that it arose spontaneously amongst those in Ireland who simply disapproved of the Rising. It

116

began to be bruited immediately after the Rising when anti-Rising British propaganda was being pumped out by Maxwell's new Irish dispensation.

The question, therefore, clearly arises: In whose interests was/is it to propagate "blood sacrifice" as a negative label?

The reality is that as a piece of brilliant hostile propaganda it belongs to the front rank. It is vivid; it has little specific meaning; it is fundamentally anti-, it is easy to remember and it can be readily associated with the target – the Rising. And, of course, its successful impact can be measured by the fact that nowadays a very broad spectrum of people unthinkingly prefer to accept its hostile connotations to the reality.

The long and the short of it is that only the British authorities, and perhaps certain Irish "Redmondites" who survived Redmond, stood, or stand, to benefit significantly from a general besmirching of the Rising.

When it comes to manipulative intelligence the British have few equals. In particular the "Blood-sacrifice" label fulfils the requirements of anti-Irish British propaganda the purpose of which was – and if we are to judge by recent articles in the British establishment press, still is – to pitch the Rising and all it represented from off the honourable and noble plinth where it properly belongs and to demean and patronise it and those involved.

By implication it lampoons Pearse and McDonagh – two poets – by implying that the Rising and everything connected with it was a futile, wrongheaded, romantic and murderous gesture.

A similar – if more focussed and immediate - technique was employed to blacken Casement whom the British wrongly believed to be the ringleader of the Rising.

So, in essence it must be said that those who disseminate the "blood sacrifice" type of hostile propaganda, either in that deliberate context, or as blind agents of the British propaganda machine, are not just ignorant, they are anti-national.

The third argument is that the Rising did not reflect the current mood of a majority of the people and should not have taken place because it wasn't part of a popular revolutionary movement, had no mandate and was "undemocratic".

As to the Rising being "undemocratic" - It is hard to know where to begin with such foolishness. The fact is that in 1916 active democracy such as we know it *simply did not exist*. The universal world order was capitalistic and exploitative imperialism, then locked in a titanic struggle for world capitalistic supremacy.

In Ireland the British variety of imperialism was reinforced by a species of colonial autocracy under the corruptly imposed Act of Union of 1801.

It should be borne in mind that even if – and it is a very notional if – Home Rule had come about the most it would have offered was something as insignificant and non-sovereign as Wales has today.

It would almost certainly have resulted in the following, as well as other restrictions; continued economic suppression, educational and social welfare deprivation, involvement in the Second World War, massive emigration, industrial stagnation and neither national nor sovereign status. No question of a Celtic Tiger.

The Proclamation of the Republic was a far-reaching democratic statement far ahead of its time, recognised widely abroad as being such.

The pursuit of (republican) sovereign independence that began in 1798 continued through the 19th century, from Emmet's magnificent failure through the Young Irelanders, the Fenians, the IRB to 1916.

It is correct to say that the Rising was the focus of all preceding republican activity and the pivot on which all subsequent separatist activity turned.

Another nonsensical hostile slogan aimed at the Rising is that it had no mandate. It must surely be the most lunatic of all the cock-eyed criticisms.

In 1916 the forum for any constitutional mandate in Ireland was the British Parliament. It seems to me somewhat improbable, to say the very least of it, that "The proposal is to have a rebellion in Ireland at Easter – All those in favour " would have made it that far, let alone been given a hypothetical mandate.

One has to wonder if in any other nation as many set out to show how clever and tolerant they are by attacking the foundations and the founding fathers of the state to which they are privileged to belong.

The Rising should not be seen either as being undemocratic or in isolation.

As to the Rising not reflecting the mood of the people and should not have taken place for that reason - of all the nonsensical arguments it is probably the most ridiculous. It should hardly be necessary to point out that the number of secret rebellions that enjoy the open support of a majority of the people before the event is very few. Indeed a major aim of the Rising was to revitalise the spirit of separate national identity in the people. To argue that the Rising did not have the support of a majority of the people in advance is absurd.

The fourth argument is the only criticism that appears to have substance. It is that The Rising should not have occurred because it could not result in military victory. But, since it is based on a total misconception of the intent and purpose of The Rising, it has no substance.

Those trying to reconstruct the past often try to carry out this engaging, if profitless and confusing, exercise by first throwing up some high-sounding slogans, such as in this context, for example: "The origin myth of the Irish State", whatever that is supposed to mean.

Having laboriously placed these straw targets, they then triumphantly knock them down again at the same time proclaiming, "Look. We told you so. We are right after all."

Well, of course, right is as right proposes and does and a fact isn't going to go away because it is told it is a myth instead.

119

The trouble with the above way of doing things is that it leaves reality out of it altogether. Instead, backed by today's sun-drenched values that cannot even take by the neck the very facts around us and shake them into coherence, it claims to be on the trail of that most ephemeral of philosophical intangibles, the Truth.

It is not a question of whether or not a rising had, or did not have, military merit, but whether the Rising that took place was adequate as to its morality, purpose, timing and effect. The answer to that is "Yes".

As quickly became clear the successful winning of public opinion was the main military achievement of the Rising. This was spectacularly demonstrated two and a half years later with the establishment of Dail Eireann, the second aim of the Rising and ratification by it of the Republic and by the War of Independence, followed by the support of a majority of the people.

Eamon Ceannt, commander of the 4th battalion of the Dublin Brigade and an important leader of The Rising, was an IRB officer who, from the outset, was a member of the Military Council that planned the Rising. His final message before his execution is a noteworthy summary of motivation for the rising:

"The enemy has not cherished one generous thought for those who, with little hope, with poor equipment and weak in numbers, withstood his forces for one glorious week. Ireland has shown that she is a nation. This generation can claim to have raised sons as brave as any that went before; and in years to come Ireland will honour those who risked their all for her honour at Easter 1916."

At the time of the Rising Padraic Pearse, the clear-headed educationalist, was thirty-seven years old, no spring chicken. Up to 1914 he had been a Home Rule supporter. As late as 1913 he appeared with Redmond on the same platform speaking in favour of it. But that year he came to reject (British) parliamentarianism as an appropriate path for the country and adopted nationalist separatism.

120

Furthermore Pearse was such a capable and efficient administrator and organiser that, within a rear of joining the Volunteers and the IRB, he had been given vital positions in both organisations over more experienced older colleagues. Hardly, one would think, the due of an impractical romantic.

In order to put the decision for a rising in 1916 into context (and, perhaps, throw some light on Connolly's insistence on a rising at that time as well as an additional reason for the date in question) it is important to take account of the fact that there was mounting concern, as pressure on the belligerents from the United States to end hostilities increased, that the war might end before a rising took place. The situation was so uncertain in the early part of that year that the British cabinet seriously considered a negotiated peace.[48]

In March General Erich von Falkenhayn (German chief-of-staff) launched the awaited battle of Verdun, the great German *putsch* that, in the footsteps of the Prussian forces forty-six years before, was intended to capture Paris and end the War. For a number of reasons, therefore, April 1916 clearly seemed to the Irish Military Council to offer most advantage for a rising and the IRB did not want to lose what seemed to be the optimum time for The Rising, and create the conditions necessary for Ireland to secure the important hearing as a belligerent nation[49].

The choices at that point were to remain *de jure* within the United Kingdom in passive compliance with the lifeless Home Rule proposals or to continue and execute the plans for The Rising.

---

[48] Greaves, op. cit, p. 41. And see also C. J. Lowe and M. L. Dockrill, *British Foreign Policy, 1914-1922, vol 2, The Mirage of Power,* London, 1972, p.238 et seq.

[49] Before the Rising Pearse emphasised that "Germany had pledged her word that if this blow" [a rising] "were struck during the war, Ireland would come into the peace terms as a belligerent'", Desmond Ryan, The Rising, p.42.

It is acknowledged by military experts, including British, that the IRB battle-plan was excellent. So far as the aims and purpose of The Rising are concerned it was a matter of strategy, timing, planning, tactics and opportunity. That it did not take place on the scale intended was not because of failure by its leaders. But in any event the achievable aims and purpose of The Rising were accomplished with the available – in men and munitions – much reduced force as spectacularly as might have been realised with a full muster of Volunteers and arms.

On the question of timing, had the Rising been attempted earlier it was likely to have failed its purpose; later and the likelihood of overseas support would have been less than it was and it would not have coincided with the German assault at Verdun. In 1916, with Germany on the crest of the war-wave, Russia, though nominally still at war with Germany, was defeated. Italy was in retreat before the Austrians. Not for another twelve months (almost to the day, on the 17th of April 1917) when the United States entered the war on the side of the Allies did the war situation show signs of any significant change.

The most notable development in that period, and well into 1918, was the massive and unexpected French counter attack at Verdun and the return to virtually static trench warfare that ensued. The Allied victory in 1918 was far from being a victory of superior troops or tactics. Nor was it, strictly speaking, a strategic victory. Germany's army was still intact and on foreign soil at nearly every point. Indeed the Germans had been victorious on most fronts and had inflicted very heavy losses. But the entry of the United States on the Allied side in 1917 was decisive. Germany's "means of waging war, physical and psychological, had been exhausted"[50]. Apart from militarily, its financial, industrial, economic, agricultural and psychological resources had been virtually bankrupted by the Allied blockade. Its people were

---

[50] *Strategy and Tactics of War,* Wilmore and Pimlott, p.12.

starving and on the point of revolt – which duly occurred. But, to quote an Anglo/Irish British general of another era, it was "a close-run thing"[51].

The reality was that "In the end Britain and France almost broke before the Germans. But for the Americans they might have"[52].

Since the Allied victory was a victory "against the run of play", although it has been read as meaning that the Allies were likely victors throughout, speculation about the Easter Rising that relies on any serious prospect of an Allied victory before 1917, is - to say the least of it - speculative.

Towards the end of 1915 the Allied war situation was not good. "The year 1915", wrote the French Marshal Joseph Joffre[53], "was dragging to a close under conditions that brought small comfort to the Allies. Our armies had everywhere been checked or beaten - the enemy appeared to have succeeded in all his undertakings". But the entry of the United States on the Allied side in 1917 was decisive.

But prior to that the situation in 1916 was otherwise. Subject only to a successful outcome of the Battle of Verdun it then looked as if the Central Powers would be in a position to negotiate a satisfactory peace settlement. The surprising success of the French counter-attack together with the intervention of the United States in 1917, changed that.

The battle of Verdun was still underway at the time of the Easter Rising.

Plan Of The Rising

What became a major problem for the leaders of The Rising in Dublin was shortage of manpower. It resulted in

---

[51] Wellington.

[52] *Strategy and Tactics of War,* Ibid.

[53] *Life of,* by G.Hanotaux and J.G.A. Fabry, 1921; See also *The Great War,* Corelli Bartnett, London, 1976

inability to adequately garrison selected positions and to maintain communications between them, which led, inevitably, to a series of unplanned sieges. The original plan did not anticipate such isolated siege development and was modified to try to cope. That meant occupation of a smaller number of strongpoints with inadequate troops and without effective overall communications. What could have been a major setback, but in fact did not at all affect the outcome, was that because of the limited turnout Volunteer posts could not adequately utilise, or lacked altogether, routes for the planned withdrawal. Disruption of the enemy's communications (by, for example, taking the telephone exchange, occupation of other vital strong points - e.g. the Castle and Trinity College - the securing of adequate means of withdrawal), all provided for in the original plan, proved impossible or very difficult. In effect, as the plan was telescoped, so was the Rising.

But the Rising is well documented and it is, therefore, unnecessary to go into more detail here than that needed in connection with the point being made.

As we know the original battle-plan provided for a nationwide uprising centred on Dublin with a withdrawal after (approximately) three-days by the Dublin units to the Shannon, linking up with troops from the west, south and north, when limited guerrilla fighting would follow before surrender. While the plan was defensive in concept, it was no less valid for that. Colonel O Neill's reference to Field-Marshal Count Helmut von Moltke's observation that: "a clever military leader will succeed in many cases in choosing defensive positions of such an offensive nature from the strategic point of view that the enemy is compelled to attack" summarised the Irish plan[54].

In a city, as in mountainous terrain, a well deployed small force, can exert pressure out of all proportion to its size on a

---

[54] Eoghan O Neill, *op. cit.*

much larger one. This is particularly the case if the larger force is not trained in street fighting and/or is badly led.

Such were the principles on which the tactics of the original plan for The Rising in Dublin were based. The intention was that a majority of the 16,000 Volunteers in the country would draw off British reinforcements from Dublin; that the German arms shipment would be landed and distributed to facilitate a short guerrilla campaign, and that Dublin would be held for a few days. It is interesting that from the outset The Rising was perceived by its planners as one of those very rare engagements where a victory for the insurgents was held to reside in tactical and moral achievement only.

Preparations were calculated on the basis that the strategically targeted buildings in Dublin would be lightly manned or empty (thus vulnerable to occupation) during the Easter holiday. The targeted buildings dominated approaches to and from the military barracks in the city and also made possible a corridor of withdrawal when that became necessary. Communication between them should also have been good. However the minimum force calculated to enable the plan to be effective was estimated to be in the region of 2,500 men.

As for the rest of the country, the German arms were to be landed at Fenit, Co. Kerry and from there the Cork, Kerry and Limerick commands would distribute them (by rail in a commandeered train) to various units of mainly unarmed Volunteers west of the Shannon. It was to be a coordinated operation ensuring safe passage for the train and secure distribution of the arms and, accordingly, the appropriate railway junctions and stations were to be taken over while road, rail and telegraph communications were also disrupted, hindering British troop movements.

Volunteer brigades to the south and west of the Shannon were to move eastwards, attacking or isolating police barracks *en route*, to the Shannon to await the Dublin units. Brigades in Cork, Belfast, Waterford would act on their own initiatives.

Because of Unionist feeling and the strength of the UVF mobilisation was considered impractical in most Ulster counties. Battalions would move into position under the guise of routine training. But secret orders for The Rising together with movement orders were issued by Pearse. Northern Volunteers would mobilise at Coalisland, Dungannon, and then move southwest to link up with the Shannon force. The combined and reasonably well-armed force would then disperse into guerrilla units and fight for as long as possible. But, and it is an important but, a prolonged guerrilla war had no part in IRB strategy.

Volunteer shortage of arms was always critical. With the debacle of the arms ship and MacNeill's countermanding orders the situation – especially outside Dublin – seemed to be disastrous. There is no doubt that had the arms been landed and distributed, had the countermanding order not been issued, a very different situation to what did occur would have resulted, particularly in Cork, Kerry and Limerick.

But such massive setbacks notwithstanding the curtailed rising succeeded in what it set out to do. To think otherwise is to fall into the foolish notion of military victory.

The Dublin of the Rising was a city of some 400,000 people, a majority of them living in the horror of what were called 'the worst slums in Europe'.

Productive work, in the sense of producing a marketable product, was almost non-existent if one discounts Guinness's brewery and Jacobs' biscuit factory. In general the only work available for men and women was servile – transport and other unskilled labour, washing, shop-keeping at the huckster level, domestic service. "... Its vast masses of unskilled labour without organisation or shield, condemned to casual jobs at coolie wages, herded into slum tenements, living eight, ten and more to a room..."[55].

---

[55] Brian O'Neill, *Easter Week*, Dublin 1936.

The *Irish Times,* later to savagely condemn the Rising and its leaders, spoke out trenchantly in February, 1914, after publication of a government enquiry into housing in the city:

We knew that Dublin had a far larger percentage of single-room tenements than any other city in the Kingdom. We did not know that nearly twenty-eight thousand of our fellow citizens live in dwellings which even the Corporation admits to be unfit for human habitation. We had suspected the difficulty of decent living in the slums; this report proves the impossibility of it. Nearly a third of our population so lives that from dawn to dark and from dark to dawn it is without cleanliness, privacy or self-respect. The sanitary conditions are revolting, even the ordinary standards of savage morality can hardly be maintained.

Wages for those living under such conditions averaged between 15 shillings and 20 shillings (approximately 20 to 25 Euro a week), with no security of tenure, and it is worth bearing in mind that this was *after* the Dublin Strike. The city no less than the country had been reduced to a wretched and non-productive dependency useful to and serving only the interests of imperial Britain. It was a situation that could not last, and one that defies the extraordinary comment that the Rising had no 'social dimension'.

It is important to appreciate a fundamental difference between the 1798 Rising and that of 1916. In the circumstances of the time in Ireland it would have been considered futile for the earlier insurrection to have been based on anything other than the idea of military victory. While recognition of constitutional principles was part of that protest, this was to be achieved – and was probably only achievable - by military rather than by moral force. But by the end of the 19th century and the first decade of the 20th the reverse was possible. Recognition of the principle and the reality of sovereignty and of social, human and constitutional rights had begun to alter the imperial mould everywhere – not least as a result of the Irish example.

Public Attitudes Prior To The Rising

To summarise:-

In 1914 the IRB had decided on a rising and, from that point forward were actively planning it in conjunction with German military and diplomatic authorities. The original plan was, as we know, for a nationwide rising. Its purpose was not to try to achieve an impossible military victory.

The intention was (i) to proclaim the Irish Republic; (ii) to revive the spirit of separatism and nationhood amongst the general public, and (iii) to fulfil the conditions required by Germany to give Ireland a hearing as a separate nation at the post war peace conference.

The public at large was probably less than well disposed to a rising, but, due to the revived cultural national outlook, to opposition to conscription, and to what was seen as 'betrayal' by Britain and by the Irish Party on the question of Home Rule, was better disposed than it might have been before 1914.

Although they had advance warnings of The Rising (through naval and military intercepts), the British all but ignored these.

Largely because of their attribution to Casement of an importance he did not have, his capture and the sinking of *Aud* reinforced the British view that even if a rising had been planned it was then neither possible nor imminent. In the light of the information at their disposal they appear to have concluded – not entirely surprisingly - that the threat of a rising had been contingent on Casement's leadership and the arms ship and that accordingly any presumed threat was nullified by his capture and by the sinking of the arms ship.

But they also took a decision that in itself might well have led to the same results as those achieved by The Rising; they decided to arrest, disarm and suppress the Volunteers after the Easter holidays. In accordance with Volunteer standing orders the effect of this would have been armed resistance anyway in which, without doubt, the IRB plan must have come into effect.

The truth is that in spite of the difficulties that suddenly and unexpectedly exploded to all but terminate the plan and as menacingly threaten it as the British, The Rising nevertheless achieved two of its three objectives, and that one was outside Irish control.

The gigantic international loss of face to the British at such a critical war-time juncture when they were moving heaven and earth to embroil the United States as their allies, should not be underestimated. They reacted with fury and brutality and with much greater focus and intelligence than they had shown up to then. It is well to bear in mind that when the centre of Dublin lay in heaps of rubble and burnt out buildings after The Rising and the Volunteers had surrendered, that British loss of face, became a feature on the international political screen and was a major factor in the "blood-sacrifice" propaganda myth, reinforced by their erroneous view of Casement's importance.

Critical Meeting

Easter Monday, 24 April, 1916 was a lovely spring day. The half deserted, cobbled streets of Dublin were free of commercial traffic and shoppers. Many of the British officers of the Dublin command, and many Dubliners, had gone to Fairyhouse races. Others enjoyed the holiday atmosphere elsewhere.

In an office in the almost deserted Dublin Castle three determined men sat in conference. They were Sir Mathew Nathan, Irish Permanent Under-Secretary, Major Price and Arthur Hamilton Norway, Secretary of the Post Office. They were finalising plans to arrest, intern or deport 600-700 Irish Volunteer, Irish Citizen Army and Sinn Fein leaders and to disarm the remainder of their few weapons.

This decision followed a week of rumour and event that included the arrest of Casement and the scuttling of the German arms ship. A list of those to be arrested was already prepared. It is impossible to overlook the likelihood that it was, or that it included, the original of the so-called 'Castle Document'.

A little considered consequence is so significant that it is hard to understand why it has not received much – if any –attention. If the Castle plan were put into effect it would have constituted the necessary *cause de guerre* for the Volunteers and armed resistance on a wide scale would inevitably have resulted.

MacNeill had already stated that such action by the British authorities would precipitate armed resistance by the Volunteers. Accordingly a rising, reactive or not, was certain to have resulted had the Castle plan gone ahead that week and arrests and attempted disarmament of the Volunteers been attempted.

But even as the orders to give the Castle plan effect were being readied these preparations were cut short by some of the first shots of the Rising. They came from the Citizen Army contingent, then at the gates, detailed to attack Dublin Castle.

Also while that critical meeting was taking place in Dublin Castle another, even more decisive meeting, had just about concluded a little more than a mile away, in Liberty Hall, headquarters of the trades union movement. It began at nine and, when it was over, the seven men who'd attended had elected Padraic Pearse President of the Provisional Government of Ireland and Commandant-General of the Army of the Irish Republic, and James Connolly, who had been so scathing of the Volunteers a few months before, vice-President and Commandant-General of the Dublin Division. Though these men did not yet know the full reality, they well understood that because of the countermand confusion instead of the twenty-five hundred or so troops The Rising plan called for, the mobilisation would be less. In

130

fact it was a mere seven hundred Volunteers, one hundred and eighteen Citizen Army men, later reinforced, surprisingly, by twelve men of the Hibernian Rifles - unexpected Redmondite, and sectarian, allies - with twelve rifles.

Street fighting, or fighting in a built-up area, clearly favoured the Irish. It is -or was - an accepted military principle that an attacker requires a minimum force three times that of a defender for any reasonable chance of success. An attacker moving through defended streets has poor observation and is vulnerable. Defenders with an all-round defence and a reserve force that can be deployed quickly as required are in a very strong position.

The original plan was to hold the line of the canals and their bridges. But, as it turned out, there was not enough manpower to take and hold all these important posts. But, to the south, the old Ringsend bridge was opened, making the road impassable. Fenian street and Mount street bridges were covered by de Valera's third battalion, Portobello bridge by outposts from St. Stephen's Green and Rialto bridge from the South Dublin Union.

The General Post Office in Sackville (O'Connell) Street became Irish HQ. The Volunteers (otherwise and later called the IRA)[56] took most of the targeted strongpoints with little difficulty, with the exception of what would prove a costly failure, Trinity College. By Monday afternoon they

---

[56] Contrary to popular opinion the term Irish Republican Army (IRA) was then a vague title used intermittently by a variety of military organisations at home and abroad since the Rising of 1798. It was first adopted by the Volunteers in 1916 which it long predated, though it was not much used until after 1919. It was not in general use in Ireland in 1916 except by "those-in-the-know". The term "IRA" came into gradual use only after the Sinn Fein convention of 1919, when the Volunteer organisation placed itself voluntarily under control of Dail Eireann.

131

effectively held the city - a temporary success. (The accompanying maps give a reasonably clear picture).

The GPO Headquarters was quickly identified by the British and from early Monday came under constant attack by rifle and machine-gun fire and by artillery bombardment from Wednesday.

The IRB plan following a logical military estimate of the situation was implemented with courage and determination. In holding the city for a week against British forces eventually amounting to the equivalent of two divisions plus artillery, accomplishing a task which might dismay a much stronger force '... the British were manoeuvred into the position that almost any course they could adopt would rebound upon themselves, and force them into contravening some of the principles of war'.[57]

The four city Volunteer battalions occupied their shortened positions and, even though battalion areas were still too big to be adequately defended by the troops available, nevertheless managed to establish outposts and secure flanks.

A brief outline indicates the revised, contracted dispositions: First Battalion, Eamon (Ned) Daly, with HQ at the Four Courts, blocked the quays and approaches from the Phoenix Park, Royal *(Collins)* and Marlborough (*McKee*) barracks and included Church street and North King street. Battalion strength was between 120 and 180 men. Original dispositions - to occupy the area bounded by the Mendicity Institute, Cabra, Broadstone and the North Dublin Union - were modified. Nevertheless a large British force was tied up until Wednesday.

Second Battalion, Thomas MacDonagh, HQ Jacobs' biscuit factory, had some 150 men and outposts in Kevin and Camden streets covering approaches from Portobello (*Cathal Brugha*) barracks, Rathmines, and linked up with Fourth

---

[57] Eoghan O Neill, op. cit.,pp.220/221.

Battalion, holding the area between it and First Battalion to block troops from Wellington (*Griffith*) Barracks.

Third Battalion, Eamon de Valera, Brigade adjutant, with a slightly smaller force (about 130 men), HQ Boland's Mills and bakery, with outposts that included Westland Row station. It also covered Grand Canal and Mount streets, Northumberland road, also commanding Beggars' Bush Barracks as well as road and rail approaches from Kingstown (Dun Laoghaire). It was intended that this battalion would help to hold open the neck of a retreat corridor to the rail routes west.

Fourth Battalion (150 men), Eamon Ceannt and his vice-Commandant, Cathal Brugha, who carved a niche for himself in the annals of Irish history before the week was out as 'the bravest of the brave', occupied the enormous South Dublin Union (now St. James's hospital), a network of buildings then covering most of the fifty-two acres they stood in, as well as Marrowbone Lane, Roe's Distillery and Watkins Brewery.

In addition was a Headquarters Battalion in the GPO of about 70 men formed by detaching small units from each of the other battalions and the Citizen Army. That number more than doubled as news of the Rising spread.

A predominantly Citizen Army contingent of about 150 men under Michael Mallin and the Countess Markievicz occupied St. Stephen's Green and the City Hall, the latter after the attack on Dublin Castle that had interrupted the meeting there. Occupation of the St. Stephen's Green park without occupying overlooking buildings was the only significant tactical error.

But the Irish were handicapped by having no supply or support systems and by having to rely on their first line ammunition only.

Had there been a full muster of the Dublin Brigade the Irish might have held an extended perimeter, maintained lines of communication within it, and occupied railway stations, keeping open their line of withdrawal while protecting their vulnerable rear at the quays and Dun

133

Laoghaire. But the shortage of troops and the consequent inability to take Trinity College, the deep-water quays at the North Wall and Amiens Street (Connolly), Westland Row (Pearse), Kingsbridge (Heuston) and Broadstone stations prevented them.

With the western quays covered by the Irish from the Mendicity Institute, the South Dublin Union, the Four Courts and other outposts, Dame street became a critical artery for a British assault.

At noon on Monday the Tricolour – the green, white and orange standard of the Republic about to be proclaimed – had been raised on the flagpole on top of the GPO building ... "The Proclamation, then posted up outside the building for the public to read, is one of the great documents of Irish history..." [58].

One of the positions occupied in Sackville (*O'Connell*) street was a wireless school (opposite the GPO, beside the Dublin Bread Company), and from here the news that "Ireland Proclaims a Republic" was flashed abroad, being received in New York and Germany even before the British learned of it.

Throughout Monday some minor fire-fights occurred with the preponderance of success going to the Irish.

The mood in the GPO headquarters of the Volunteers that evening was one of jubilation. So far they had done well. The Republic had been proclaimed to the world. They had inflicted casualties on the enemy, receiving few themselves. They held the positions they'd occupied and, surely, the rest of the country was 'out' by now too. But that could not be established. Communications with the rest of the country was virtually nil. That assumption that the country was 'out' was, in the main, wrong.

---

[58] *The Civil War,* 1922-23, p.15. See also Appendix 2.

British Dispositions

The British held nine barracks around Dublin stretching in a semi-circle from the Bull Island, to the north of the city, to Merrion, almost directly opposite across Dublin Bay in the south, confining the city between them and the sea. At each extremity were a Bombing School at Merrion's Elm Park (now a golf club), and a Musketry school at Dollymount (now also a golf club) on the Bull Island. Between were Beggars' Bush Barracks, between Northumberland and Shelbourne roads; Portobello (*Cathal Brugha*) Barracks near the canal in lower Rathmines; Wellington *(Griffith)* Barracks on the South Circular Road; Richmond Barracks, at Islandbridge; The Royal Hospital, Kilmainham; Islandbridge Barracks; Military Headquarters at Parkgate; Marlborough Barracks *(McKee)*; Arbour Hill; Royal Barracks (*Collins*); Ship Street Barracks beside the Castle and the RIC Barracks in Phoenix Park (now Garda Headquarters). Of these, four were strongly garrisoned and dominated approaches to the city centre.

About 2,500 British troops occupied these barracks. There were some 6,000 mobile combat troops in the rest of the country.

When it came the British response was capable and effective. As soon as The Rising was confirmed British troops were rushed to Dublin. The GOC Irish Command, Major-General Lovick Bransby Friend, was on leave in England; Brigadier W.H.M. Lowe was in the Curragh.

On Monday afternoon the Curragh 1,600-man stand-to mobile column was ordered to Dublin, together with another thousand men from the 3rd Reserve Cavalry Brigade, who followed on Tuesday, all under Brigadier Lowe who took temporary command in Dublin.

When Field-Marshal Lord French, GOC British Home Forces, received news of the Rising he immediately ordered additional units to Ireland, which would bring the British strength in Dublin to 16,000. Another full division (the 60th) was brought to stand-to in Britain. On Tuesday troops from

135

Belfast and the Curragh had already brought British fighting strength in Dublin to more than 6,500. A battery of 18-pounder field-guns was ordered up from Athlone.

By Wednesday reinforcements from Britain brought the number of effectives in the city, together with additional artillery, close to 12,000. They quickly identified and isolated the main Irish strongpoints. As Gen. Halley put it: 'The British had made up their minds to blot out the headquarters as quickly as possible and it was sound tactics to do so'[59].

Having made his dispositions French arranged a meeting with Redmond who briefed him as best he could, presumably in the depressing knowledge that his star was waning. Whatever support he still possessed from the Irish people would soon pass from his hands forever.

French appointed Major General Sir John Maxwell GOC, Ireland. Like Kitchener, 'Bloody' Maxwell had served much of his career in Egypt, but had also, in 1902, served in Ireland on the staff of the Duke of Connaught.

On Friday he issued a proclamation which included:- "If necessary, I shall not hesitate to destroy all buildings within any area occupied by rebels, and I warn all persons within the area specified below, and now surrounded by His Majesty's troops, forthwith to leave such areas... all other men who present themselves at the said examining post must surrender unconditionally, together with any arms and ammunition in their possession."

He had a pit capable of accommodating 100 corpses dug in the grounds of Kilmainham jail with, as events were to show, the firm resolve to fill it 'if necessary'.

The dramatic story of the Rising is well documented and the narrative lies outside our scope here. It is enough to say that the fighting, some of it both bloody and brave, lasted until Saturday[60].

---

[59] op.cit.

[60] A detailed account of Easter Week will be found in the author's *Birth of a Republic*.

136

The battle reduced the centre of Dublin to ruins. The Volunteers demonstrated their skill and determination by holding up and decimating with their small forces large units of the British Army. At noon on Saturday Pearse and his colleagues decided that it was time to surrender. Their struggle had lasted longer and was far more successful than they had had any right to expect. It was now to hope that it would serve its purpose and achieve its objectives.

Elizabeth O'Farrell was one of the small number of brave women of Cumann na mBan (Company of Women) who had accompanied the men throughout the battle and had exposed herself to enemy fire. Pearse now asked if, under a flag of truce, she would contact the British commander and tell him they wished to discuss terms for surrender.

It was a dangerous mission. A short while before they had seen a local family of four, parents and two daughters, shot down by the enemy as they fled their burning home carrying white flags. Miss O'Farrell was determined to do what she could.

A white flag was held out. There was an immediate burst of fire and it was withdrawn. On the third attempt there was no fire and Miss O'Farrell ventured into the street holding it aloft. She walked towards the British barricade at the other end at approximately 12.45 p.m., to be taken into custody and held in, of all places, Tom Clarke's shop[61]. She was treated as a spy by 'a very truculent and panicky colonel' (Ryan, op. cit), searched and interrogated until Brigadier Lowe arrived from his HQ in Trinity. Lowe interviewed her and was courteous but refused to treat except on the basis of unconditional surrender, failing which hostilities would recommence within half an hour.

---

[61] His shop had been an IRB meeting place for years. Tom Clarke, a relatively old man and a former Fenian who had spent years in a British prison hulk, was very active in reviving the IRB in the early years of the century. He was one of those held responsible by the British for the Rising.

Miss O'Farrell returned with this message. At 3.30 p.m., she and Pearse met Lowe to whom Pearse surrendered, handing his sword to Brigadier Lowe.

Pearse then wrote out the following order:

In order to prevent the further slaughter of Dublin citizens, and in the hope of saving the lives of our followers now surrounded and hopelessly out-numbered, the members of the Provisional Government present at Headquarters have agreed to an unconditional surrender, and the Commandants of the various districts in the City and Country will order their commands to lay down arms.

P.H.PEARSE
29 April 1916, 3.45 p.m.

Connolly added:

"I agree to these conditions for the men only under my own command in the Moore Street district and for the men in the Stephen's Green command"[62].

If it were further necessary to de-bunk the "blood-sacrifice" hocus-pocus, this document is clear. The unconditional surrender was specifically made to save lives, not to waste them in pointless sacrifice.

Over the next forty-eight hours, even where fighting still continued, Miss O'Farrell brought this order to the various Irish commands.

---

[62] Another version of a surrender order came up for sale in May, 2005. It is presumably a second, later order. While the wording is similar, it differs in a number of important respects including the date – 30th April, 1916 and that it is alleged to have been written from Arbour Hill Prison *after* Pearse's surrender. It does not include the addendum by Connolly. It runs:-
"In order to prevent further slaughter of the civil population and in the hope of saving the lives of our followers, the members of the Provisional Government present at Headquarters have decided on an unconditional surrender, and Commandants or officers commanding districts will order their commands to lay down arms. P. H. Pearse, Dublin, 30th April 1916."

At that point a strange and unreal quiet, like some felt but unseen cloud of suspense, now fell over the city. From the rubble that had been Sackville street a great pall of smoke that would linger for days rose silent and menacing into an azure sky. This disturbing and suspenseful quiet, lacking all sense of the tranquillity normally associated with a calm and gentle Spring day, was broken from time to time by the sound of a rifle shot or the staccato hammer of a Vickers gun. The Rising was all but over.

The last outposts to surrender were those of MacDonagh in Jacobs and de Valera in Boland's Mills.

It is from this point that the hostile mythology begins. Another apocryphal story, broadcast in relation to the prisoners who were marched through the streets to their deaths or imprisonment, is that the citizens of Dublin reviled and spat – or worse – at them.

This was, perhaps, the case in some areas of suburbia and, more understandably, where British war wives and widows congregated. But it was self-evidently – as the passing days convincingly witnessed – very far from the norm, though, like the other disparaging, 'blood-sacrifice', fiction, it, too, has come to be accepted as the overriding truth.

The words of a Canadian journalist, F. A. McKenzie – himself no lover of the Irish insurgents - who witnessed the surrender and the guarded columns of marching prisoners, speak eloquently for themselves:

'I have read many accounts of public feeling in Dublin in these days. They are all agreed that the open and strong sympathy of the mass of the population was with the British troops. That this was so in the better parts of the city, I have no doubt. But certainly what I myself saw in the poorer districts did not confirm this. It rather indicated that there was a vast amount of sympathy with the Rebels, particularly after the Rebels were defeated.'[63]

---

[63] McKenzie, *The Irish Rebellion*, London, 1916, p.92 et seq.

McKenzie describes people cheering a column of Irish soldiers under guard, some of them women, singing a song in Irish as they marched between lines of British troops near Dublin Castle on the Sunday evening following surrender.

Provinces

The situation in the provinces was different and never developed as planned. The disaster of *Aud*; the confusion resulting from the orders and counter-orders from Dublin, and failure of communications - also partly the result of the confusion and partly due to the inability of the Volunteers to take and control telephone and telegraph centres in Dublin - caused The Rising and movement to the line of the Shannon to be aborted.

But limited mobilisation did take place in some areas, particularly in Wexford and Galway, in Wexford with some success. Under Robert Brennan, Liam Etchingham, Seamus Doyle and Seamus Rafter, and acting on verbal orders from Dublin, 600 Volunteers seized and established headquarters in Enniscorthy. Railway lines were cut and the towns of Ferns and Gorey were occupied. But it was too little and too late.

The British dispatched a force of 1,000 infantry and 70 cavalry in a crude armoured train against Enniscorthy, but news of the surrender in Dublin arrived before hostilities began.

Similar limited actions occurred in Limerick and Galway – where a British destroyer shelled notional Volunteer positions, the result being more holes in the Connemara bogs. In Leinster minor mobilisations also took place in Louth and Kildare. In Cork and Kerry, which figured so significantly in the subsequent War of Independence, there was little activity, in the case of latter county resulting mainly from the capture and sinking of *Aud*. In Cork city, surrounded by hills, the British trained artillery on the city from these trapping the Volunteers under their muzzles. It

140

took Cork some three years to overcome the implied stigma, when it became the premier fighting county in the War of Independence (1919-1921).

Atrocities

During the fighting in Dublin some British troops were guilty of atrocities against civilians, mainly in North King street and the area of the Four Courts. In one block of houses nine men and boys, none with any connection with the Rising, were murdered in their homes. On the other side of the street four men were dragged from their firesides and bayoneted. In all fifteen innocent men and boys were murdered, some were tortured.

A number of people were shot while carrying white flags, and civilians were killed and wounded by sniper fire, many in their own homes. The official figures for those killed or wounded in the Rising is 1,351. The number of Irish soldiers killed has not been determined, but Dorothy Macardle[64] gives it as fifty-six and Ryan (op. cit) as sixty-one. He adds that this figure is incomplete. He puts the number of wounded at between 100 and 120.

MacNeill's countermanding order has, over and over, been held up as the principal reason why the Rising wasn't on a bigger scale. It undoubtedly played a part. But the loss of *Aud* (and the capture of Casement) were of at least equal and possibly of greater significance. Without the arms shipment the rising of the south and west was prejudiced and the plan to break out from Dublin and hold the line of the Shannon thwarted.

Some might argue that the decision to go ahead in these circumstances was foolhardy. The fact remains that The Rising, curtailed as it was, nevertheless achieved – spectacularly, as events demonstrated – all its achievable objectives; namely the reviving of national spirit and the Proclamation of the Republic

---

[64] *The Irish Republic.*

with, contrary to the 'blood-sacrifice' theme, little loss of life. The third objective was not achievable in any event.

Often overlooked by commentators on the Rising is the fact that even if the arms and munitions from *Aud* had been successfully landed and distributed, even if there had been no countermanding order and resulting confusion and small muster, and if The Rising had gone ahead on the scale originally intended, it could not have achieved more than it did – and, in that case, almost certainly with greater loss of life.

In further and, it can be said, final contradiction of the improper "blood-sacrifice" fiction, the mood of the people changed dramatically within weeks of the Rising. The Volunteers and their executed leaders were hailed as heroes. In great and increasing numbers the people, assessed what had occurred, recognised that it and those who took part in it had acted in their name, and endorsed the Rising. The revolutionary climate of thought necessary to procure a forceful and compelling challenge to alien rule was launched and well underway.

Executions

The first executions of its leaders took place on Wednesday, 3 May, four days after The Rising. They continued at intervals over the next two weeks.

It seems appropriate to finally put the mare's nest of false 'blood-sacrifice' idea out of its misery:-

The reference in the Proclamation of the Republic, read by Pearse at noon on Monday 24th April, 1916, to 'gallant allies in Europe' is an indication of the extent of planning involved.

In April, 1922, Cathal Brugha, who was to die tragically two months later on the outbreak of civil war, published in the Easter edition of *Poblacht na h-Eireann* a summary of part of the plan of the Rising for Dublin. It included the following: "Connolly it was who prepared the plan for the

142

defence of Dublin. Strong positions between the city and the various military barracks that almost surrounded it were to be seized by the Volunteers. The one in the city itself (Ship street) was to be dominated by the seizure of certain strong buildings in its vicinity. A human chain was to link up such strongholds with others. There was to be an open chain from the Liffey to Clontarf and Fairview up to Phibsboro. Over this space a mobile force was to be concentrated. The defence was to be carried out by the Volunteers and the Citizen Army acting together.

"The successful holding of the city for a certain time was based on the assumption that at least 1,500 would participate. (In view of accepted military opinion that it would have required a minimum of approximately 2,500 men to make the plan fully effective this may be an error deriving from the actual turnout.) Arrangements were made in various parts of the country to rise simultaneously".[65]

In the section dealing with The Rising the official German naval history of the war (translation in *An t-Oglach,* July, 1926), makes it clear that the German view was that a rising would i/ affect British morale, ii/ divert British forces from the Western front and iii/ make available submarine bases or depots on the west coast of Ireland.

Colonel O Neill writes:- 'The occupation of the city had a strategic as well as a tactical significance. A battle for its possession had a strategic as well as a tactical aim.'

While the leaders did not envisage military victory or independence -- and it is futile to postulate theories on such an assumption -- a significant rising was a necessary strategic requirement to achievement of the planned design. As we know the battle-plan was defensive, but no less valid for that.

It is not, therefore, a question of whether a rising had, or did not have, merit. The question is was the Rising that took

---

[65] The statement that the plan was prepared by Connolly overstates the case, but helps confirm that it was finalised during the days he spent in January with the Military Council of the IRB and about which he was afterwards so secretive.

143

place adequate as to purpose, timing and effect[66]. In any case, had the Rising not pre-empted the planned British swoop and arrests that same week, a reactive rising in accordance with Volunteer policy of resistance to any such attempt was inevitable.

Colonel O Neill again: "The proclamation of the Republic stressed the historic right of the Irish nation to independence ... The Rising was to be in defence of that right ... not by attacking the British garrisons directly, but by seizing certain points openly in the name of the Irish nation and defending them openly against the inevitable British attack".

Ryan says: "The Cork, Clare, Tipperary and West-Limerick Volunteers were to seize railways and barracks in their immediate areas, disarm the police, surround Limerick and march into the relief of the city battalions. The plan assumed that the ... arms train with the arms from *Aud* landed at Fenit would pass without interference by police or military..." [67].

A question raised by Major Gen. P.F. Nowlan, sometime Assistant Army Chief-of Staff, with the author is:- "What rations did the Volunteers muster with? In other words how long did they expect to be in the field?"

So far as it is possible to ascertain the (different) mobilisation orders to the Volunteers and Citizen Army specified one, two and three days field rations. Taken together with other evidence – for instance the fact that Sean Heuston was ordered to hold the Mendicity Institute for only

---

[66] On this question Brian Murphy writes:- "In English denial of Home Rule one finds the source of justification for the action of Pearse. Ireland had not received, and could not expect to receive, fair treatment from England ... What, if the promises were not to be trusted, and the land itself to be divided? That, indeed, was the reality of the situation in 1916. The Rising may not have been wanted, but it was needed if the promised land of Ireland's historic aspirations was to be secured " (op cit., p.58).

[67] Ryan, op. cit., p. 88.

144

a matter of hours and held out for days; that orders were for three-day manoeuvres similar to those carried out a year earlier and, of course, the German requirement - then the theory that a Rising was intended to last at least three, possibly four, days seems likely and would, therefore, have taken the matter of appropriate pack- and field-rations into account.

The ration orders suggest that the leaders did not anticipate holding out in Dublin for much longer than three or four days and that this was considered sufficient to achieve the strategic objective for the post war peace conference.

Munitions were a problem. The Dublin Volunteers were restricted to front-line ammunition only. In the south and west, where the main body of troops were to hold the Shannon line, reliance for arms and munitions was principally on those expected from *Aud*.

It is therefore probably safe to conclude that the Rising was planned to last three/four days in Dublin, followed by the planned withdrawal.

In the event the Rising in Dublin surpassed all expectations. The extended period of action in Dublin should probably be seen less as a planned tactic than one of circumstance and opportunity. Because of the small turnout it was not possible for the Dublin Volunteers to hold open the withdrawal routes to the western rail stations, to take and hold the stations themselves and to maintain effective, or any, communications with the rest of the country, resulting in a fundamental change of plan, but not of objective.

"As to the projected plans, it is obvious that the present time is inopportune to disclose them. Suffice it to say that they were carefully prepared months ahead, every detail that would ensure success and co-ordination being worked out"[68]. The extent of the plan may be gauged from the fact that it

---

[68] Brian O'Higgins the *Wolfe Tone Annual,* 1946 p.98, from an unpublished document by Liam Mellowes (executed during the civil war, 1922).

included many aspects of civil government, including the issue of stamps.

Had there not been one in 1916 a rising would certainly have taken place sooner or later, perhaps during the 20s or 30s – if not, certainly during the course of the Second World War.

Again it is not, therefore, a question of whether the idea of a rising did or did not have merit, but whether The Rising that took place succeeded.

The Rising was the essential pivot on which the whole movement for national sovereignty swung. From its ashes, phoenix-like, grew and spread a national unity of purpose more powerful and single-minded than anything that preceded it since the Union.

It became quickly clear that Clausewicz's third aim of war was the main military achievement of the Rising. This was spectacularly demonstrated two years later with the annihilation of the IPP at the polls, the establishment of Dail Eireann and ratification by it of the Republic declared in 1916.

'The defensive areas chosen by the Irish were excellent ... Irish officers were well trained and all had specialised in street fighting as a military subject ... individually [they] were superior as soldiers to the ... 59th British (North Midland) Division. Their greatest weakness after shortage of manpower, and it cannot be attributed to that alone, was poor communications. They "suffered at all times from lack of information."[69]

After the Rising all, indeed, changed utterly. But it was not, as is often thought, a change in the attitude of the Irish alone. The change in British administration was total and nation-wide.

From the civil, more-or-less benign, "caretaker administration" of Birrel and Nathan that had meandered carelessly along in the years before 1916 it was transformed, in a matter of days, into a repressive and coercive military

---

[69] Halley, *op. cit.*

administration under a military governor with strict martial law, curfew and intimidation across most of the country.

Within weeks of the Rising, Maxwell recorded:

"Censored correspondence of interned prisoners ... shows a decided turn for the worse. Whereas at first their letters were humble and apologetic, now the tone has become defiant, and shows that they think themselves national heroes... There is a growing feeling that out of rebellion more has been got than by constitutional methods, hence Mr. Redmond's power is on the wane".

It seems fitting to conclude , with the words of one of the belittled leaders and poets who, besides being the most poetic in appearance, was also the military prodigy who drafted the initial plans for the Rising; Joseph Mary Plunkett.

The first stanza of his poem THIS HERITAGE TO THE RACE OF KINGS, is:

This heritage to the race of kings
Their children and their children's seed
Have wrought their prophecies in deed
Of terrible and splendid things.

THE THIRD MYTH

Why Civil War After
The Pact?

THE THIRD MYTH

Why Civil War After The Pact?

OF THESE THREE EMBEDDED MYTHS the third and most recent is also both the most perplexing and the least difficult to explain. This arises, at least in part, from the fact that it has, for long, been subordinate to partisan argument and a reluctance - by those who should - to assess and examine the circumstances that gave rise to it – and who have, thus, negatively contributed to the confusion.

Civil war is not about conquest or economics. It is about what faction will govern the nation. There are no winners. All are losers, with strong and differing perspectives - the victors claiming the moral high ground and denigrating their opponents.

On May 24 1923, the civil war that had racked the new State for eleven months, sundering families, friendships, comrades-in-arms and the unity of purpose of the War of Independence, ended in a cease fire. Predictably, the victorious pro-Treaty Irish Free State Government promoted themselves as sole upholders of the illusory "right".

But that was then. Today it is disheartening to find Free State propaganda and reactive denunciation from adherents of the other side still being advanced.

The central and significant question is: Why did civil war break out only one month after the far-reaching and percipient Collins/deValera Pact had been agreed?[70]

The Pact was a profoundly significant and promising agreement. Nevertheless, the civil war that scarred the nation and the body politic of the neophyte state physically and morally for generations to come exploded just thirty-nine days after it was agreed.

To this day the reasons for this dramatic reversal remain disputed and, as a result, clouded and controversial. Without recourse to reason, knowledge or understanding political legatees blame each other retrospectively. So readily does the appropriate question seem to have fallen – or perhaps been dropped – into a deep and misleading rut on the road of recent Irish history and so convincingly does it accommodate to pre-digested accepted opinion, that the idea of disinterring it with the object of reasonable reassessment tends to be brushed aside in favour of the disputatious and uncritical views that the victors' version of events must be entirely right; or, failing that, that of the defeated must be – a more difficult doctrine since "the victors are always right"..

But, while the victors' case is *not* always right the case of the defeated is usually just as biased. What is clear is that the time for avoiding the question, if that were ever valid, is now long past.

---

[70] The foregoing question is the last significant one relating to the civil war that corroded the fabric of the new state even before it was established. The terms of the Pact sought to eliminate the increasing threat of civil war and to establish political accord and constitutional progress. These aims were to be achieved by forming a Sinn Fein Coalition (republican) Government, reunited from both sides to the Treaty dispute, that would govern under the Treaty and a new constitution.

A refocusing on factors – some of which may even at first glance seem to be unrelated - coupled with the overall context, circumstances and sequence, helps give a clearer picture than the usual fudge. The correlation of what have often –incorrectly - been seen as *isolated* facts helps us come to a reasonably clear assessment of that intense month between the Pact and the outbreak of civil war that accommodates to the reality of the period.

The prevalent tendency to judge the past by the standards of today, forcing facts out of their time, often provides additional distortion.

Such distortions – unwitting or not – strike deeper than the history books. They affect public perceptions about the people - and their ideals – who helped found the state. They are all the more regrettable when they emanate from those whose responsibility it is to know and to do better. More regrettable is that those of younger generations with limited access to the facts accept such distortions from either side.

Background

The Pact was agreed over May 18th, 19th, 20th 1922. Ironically, important details that should help clarify what happened between then and the outbreak of the civil war have usually been ignored or left to hang isolated and out of context, thus contributing to the overall lack of clarity.

The civil war itself (the source of our two major political parties), is now well documented and understood. Nevertheless, even today the reasons for it and the breakdown of the Pact that could have prevented it remain extraordinarily clouded, controversial and contentious.

The absence of any adequate history of the period between the Pact and the outbreak of the civil war has been compared to the similar absence of information - on a much larger scale - about the civil war before my book *The Civil*

War in Ireland was published in the mid-1960s[71]. Incredibly it was the first – and for some time thereafter the only – book on this very important historical event. Up to then the civil war period, 1922-1923 – and up to 1926 - was an historical blank. Irish history stopped dead at the beginning of 1922 after the signing of the Treaty and resumed again just as suddenly in or about 1927. So far as the teaching and understanding of modern, formative, Irish history was concerned the intervening years and the events that filled them might as well not have happened.

Similarly, today, instead of a correct and unadulterated answer to the question:- *Why did civil war break out only a month after an agreement was reached by the political leaders of both sides,* there are only blank or biased inherited explanations from adherents of both sides to the civil war, without too much regard to fact, each blaming the other for what happened.

Surprisingly enough our search for answers begins with the Anglo-Irish Treaty negotiations of autumn, 1921. An outline of events between the aftermath of The Rising and these negotiations helps put things in proper relation to one another.

After The Rising the extraordinary upsurge of nationalist fervour all over the country fulfilled the IRB planners' hopes and expectations. It seemed as if the people, having been trapped on a kind of political roundabout from which it was possible to see little except generally alien impressions that substituted for constitutional substance, had succeeded in bringing this disorderly whirligig to a halt and begun the business of a unified move towards republican reality.

Public reaction to the executions of the leaders of The Rising and to the hanging of Roger Casement had been deep. This was further inflamed by the wholesale arrest and, in many cases, deportation to detention camps and jails in Wales and England, of hundreds of Volunteers and Sinn Fein

---

[71] Published in 1966, it was the pioneering book on the subject.

members. And, of course – as in England itself - there was powerful and hostile reaction to the British proposals for conscription.

The release and homecoming of many of the prisoners at the end of 1916 and in 1917 provided impetus to the increasingly strong national feeling in the country, so that, in spite of the fact that forty-seven of them were in jail, and of serious intimidation and harassment by the authorities, Sinn Fein could put forward seventy-three candidates for the 1918 Westminster general election. There were 105 Irish seats and in some cases a Sinn Fein candidate ran for election in more than one constituency.

Though standing on an abstentionist ticket the result was astonishing; without representation of any kind before the election, not only did every Sinn Fein candidate take a seat, they literally wiped the Irish Political Party – if not its influence, as we shall see - off the political map. From having held 68 seats before the election, the IPP returned six.

It was a profound demonstration by the people of support for a national constitutional programme and Sinn Fein were galvanised by this remarkable victory and wholehearted endorsement. The leaders set about forming a native government, the first since Grattan's parliament of the 18th century and the first-ever democratic parliament of Ireland representative of the popular will of the people, Dail Eireann.

Its first meeting was in January 1919.

The Irish election results dismayed and disquieted the government of the United Kingdom, which, it seems, discerned therein the first glimmerings of a greater threat – that to the Empire itself (which in fact it was)[72].

Of the election results Ronald McNeill (Lord Cushendun) wrote:

---

[72] Over the next three years that threat would become stronger and spread to some of the other colonies, in particular to India.

155

"The general election of 1918 revealed that the whole of Nationalist Ireland had gone over with horse, foot and artillery, with bag and baggage, from the camp of so-called Constitutional Home Rule, to the Sinn Feiners, who made no pretence that their aim was anything short of complete independent sovereignty for Ireland."

The British response included prohibition of the Dail and its members and, significantly, the hurried preparation and drafting of the Government of Ireland Act, which was, if you like, a sort of vicarious Home Rule. Its compound intention included providing *de jure* status to Northern Ireland as a separate (if undefined) area within the United Kingdom. It would, moreover, profoundly affect the treaty two years on. The Act came into force in 1920, purporting to provide for two governments in Ireland, a southern and a northern – as classic an example of legalized "Divide and Conquer" as may be found. Its primary purpose was to anticipate the possible need to safeguard British strategic interests by copper-fastening the north of Ireland within the United Kingdom. Except for Unionists the Irish electorate totally rejected the Act.

In the meantime the Irish War of Independence began in 1919, and developed. It lasted for two and a half years during which period the will and determination of the people for freedom and independence was demonstrated in one of the 20th centuries' classic guerrilla campaigns against a foreign occupying power.

In places, particularly in Cork and other parts of Munster, Irish forces achieved remarkable successes. But the cost was considerable. When captured Irish soldiers were not treated as prisoners of war and were liable to summary execution. But it was on the civilian population that the main burden fell, particularly after terrorist forces, the Black and Tans and the inappropriately named Auxiliary Police Cadets (the 'Auxies'), fell ravenously on a country under martial law. There was a huge military presence all over the militarised zones; towns, villages and homes, even - as in Cork - vast city areas, were razed and burnt to the ground. Subjugation by terror became the order of the day.

At the height of the War, May, 1921, in a startling example of dysfunctional electoral procedure, a British inspired election intended to ratify the two parliaments of the Government of Ireland Act was held in Ireland. It spectacularly backfired.

In that election Sinn Fein's success was even greater than it had been in the general election of 1918. It won all the contestable 124 seats. As a result the second Dail Eireann assumed its (still proscribed) office on August 16th, 1921. But by then, as a preliminary to negotiations, a truce had been arranged.

Negotiations were prolonged and difficult and were largely characterised by indecision and irresoluteness from British prime-minister Lloyd George and his cabinet. But a truce was finally agreed on 11th July, 1921. It was a respite some thought might be followed by peace and self-determination. After further long and complex negotiations it was eventually agreed that discussions – the treaty negotiations – would begin in the autumn.

A crucial point that would profoundly affect the Collins/deValera Pact of the following year became evident during the preparatory exchanges. It was, and hinged on, the British attitude to republicanism.

As if governed by an article of faith carved in stone the British adopted a non-negotiable position on the question of republicanism, simply refusing, point-blank, to acknowledge or to treat with Dail Eireann or its republican nature. Within a twelvemonth, as we shall see, this attitude would bear bloody and baneful fruit and have disastrous long-term effects in Ireland.

Republicanism in any form, good, bad or indifferent was not to be tolerated. Though the Irish had a *de facto,* elected legislative republican assembly and cabinet, the British refused to recognise or treat with the Irish delegation as its representatives, or with an Irish Republic.

Their stance was that the treaty negotiations derived substance and status from the Government of Ireland Act and that that was the legislative base for negotiation.

As we know the Act purported to provide for two Irish parliaments to govern the – as yet undivided - country, North and South. A second – indeed perhaps the primary - purpose was to secure British strategic interests in Ireland, an attitude adopted with the undiluted self-assurance that is the timeless hall-mark of those whom chance and circumstance have placed at the political heart of mighty empires and who, with hands encased in either velvet or mail, assume the direction of international destinies.

It follows, of course, that it is their opinions and purposes that are to be taken as the right and to which opposition is not simply rebellion, but is morally unwarrantable. It is a viewpoint that gives rise to a tendency, amongst even the most liberal and enlightened subjects of powerful nations when observing the customs and habits of others, to do so from the standpoint that their perspective is - by the fact alone of being powerful – also correct and superior.

Such was the spirit, perfectly enshrined in Lord Palmerston's dictum that "Great powers – " in this instance Britain "- have neither permanent friends nor permanent enemies, only interests", in which Britain, in 1921, approached negotiations with the Irish people.

Whatever the Irish themselves thought or held, their position was that the Irish delegation derived such legal status as they might have from the parliament provided for under the British 1920 Government of Ireland Act. It followed, therefore, that the Northern Ireland Government also had the right of participation. But the Northern parliament refused to attend or to send representatives to the negotiations.

On the other hand, except for Unionists, the Irish had rejected the Act and, the British point of view notwithstanding, were and considered themselves to be delegates of Dail Eireann. A further complication was that the Irish leaders - the existence of republican Dail Eireann notwithstanding – understood that an independent, sovereign and separate republic could not result from these negotiations. (It was also understood, though it was hoped such an outcome could be avoided, that because of internal differences, Sinn Fein could well divide into Government and Opposition). Furthermore, while the delegation was divided on the question, the Dail Cabinet did not consider that a Treaty would be concluded on signing alone and must be ratified by Dail Eireann.

But British view was that on signature (in tense circumstances later described by Michael Collins as "the duress of the facts") and irrespective of the Irish position, the Treaty was, by the fact alone of the delegates signing, conclusive. So, while the British viewed the Treaty as finalised on signing, the Irish did not.

Primary constitutional positions of both sides were ignored – by the British in denying the existence of Dail Eireann, and by the Irish in ignoring the Government of Ireland Act. There were, therefore, on signing radically different views in Dublin and in London regarding the status of the agreement. Instead of resolving, or at least diminishing, the Irish constitutional dilemma, the Treaty formula became instead a source of further serious and growing confusion.

Reasons for British concern about republicanism are not difficult to discern. Although they were on the victor side, the War had cost them dear; war debts were horrendous, unemployment was rife and social unrest was as bad as it had been in the years before the war. In addition they were still involved in unwanted military expeditions – in the middle east, where the prizes, then as now, were rich and in Russia, against the Soviet republic, where there were no prizes at all. And now here was that political ogre 'republic' again squatting on their very doorstep!

But, and in some ways most disturbing, the geopolitical norm of the entire 'civilised' world, clear and defined

159

throughout the 19th century and earlier, had been stricken to its roots. Great empires that had provided a universally understood and, it had seemed, unshakeable political and economic order, with centuries of development behind them, had simply vanished in the space of a few years. They may have been empires with which, from time to time, Britain had differences in the struggle for 'world order', but they shared with her a common perception of how things ought to be. Of that mighty and elegant society only the fragile British Empire – the youngest of those great imperial conglomerates – was the solitary survivor. Worst of all some of the others, now no more, had fallen – or were about to fall - beneath the common boot and denomination of 'republic'.

For, not alone had the war brought about the disintegration of empires, it had also thrust republicanism to the forefront of world political activity, with the United States, republic and creditor nation, leading the way. Before the war there had been only two major republics, one on either side of the Atlantic with both of which Britain had been at war, including a war of Independence, within the imperial term. And now, so close, Britain's own political stability was threatened by that self-same republicanism!

Throughout the 19th century treaties in Europe tended in the main to be in the nature of more or less temporary alliances of economic/military advantage. The British government were well aware that a treaty with a republican Ireland would be no such "temporary little arrangement", but a significant dent in its own strategic, economic and tactical defences.

It is, therefore, clear that the idea of republicanism was much more than a catch-call from an agitated Irish peasantry. It was a threat to all that the British Empire represented; on no account must it be allowed to burgeon within the orbit of the United Kingdom; not at any price – certainly not under the hand of Irish separatists.

But, as Napoleon observed at the Peace of Amiens in 1802: "Between old monarchies and a young republic the spirit of hostility must always exist".

Here is the root of the absolute refusal by the British to recognise either republican Dail Eireann or the Irish delegates to the negotiations as its official representatives.

Another important factor is that Dail Eireann was - unusually at any time, but particularly so then - a mono-party assembly consisting solely of Sinn Fein deputies. Had it been other than an assembly created in unusual circumstances and claiming – with considerable legitimacy - to be a national parliament, it would almost certainly have by then included an Opposition[73]. But with the need for vital treaty negotiations recognised by Britain and about to begin, now arose this curious political phenomenon. Dail Eireann, the elected government - if admittedly unconventionally - of the Irish people, charged to negotiate on their behalf, was refused recognition by those who were about to negotiate with its delegates.

The result was a stalemate. But, then, after weeks of fruitless preliminary exchanges, Lloyd George came up with an equivocal formula that enabled negotiations to begin. It cleverly excluded any reference to Dail Eireann or to republicanism, while at the same time allowing room for the idea of some form of Irish independence. This was the formula: "How the association of Ireland with the community of nations known as the British Empire may best be reconciled with Irish National aspirations."

Accordingly, on this equivocal basis, discussions opened in London on October 11th, 1921.

---

[73] The yeast binding many shades of opinion from Left to Right across the political spectrum and holding Sinn Fein together as one party, was the principle of self-determination. It had brought them together. Its fulfilment, particularly in part, would inevitably, in the political scheme of things, lead to political division sooner or later.

Additional confusion arose from the fact that, while the British refused to recognise the republic or to negotiate on the basis of "nation and nation", the Irish delegates never relinquished the position that they had been appointed by Dail Eireann and were answerable to it.

Clearly preparations for the negotiations by both sides were made in what might be described as a thick fog of discord. Each side could not, or would not, acknowledge the position of the other. But, inasmuch as Lloyd George's formula enabled talks to begin it was worthwhile; insofar as it enabled the parties to shut their eyes to important realities, it was flawed and had far-reaching and awful consequences.

Fraught with drama and heartache, the negotiations continued until 6th December. The neophyte Irish delegation, facing what was one of the most powerful, experienced and ruthless teams of negotiators of the 20th century[74], was quickly wrong-footed. Towards the end the Irish delegation had been so divided that, after its final meeting with the Dail cabinet before signing, its members returned to London in separate groups.

The treaty was signed in the small hours of December 6th, 1921, under the threat of signing or of "immediate and terrible war"; Collins's "duress of the facts".

There is no need here to go into the controversy surrounding the signing which is well and comprehensively documented[75]. But for our purpose it is necessary both to outline the sequence of events between the signing and the Collins/deValera Pact in the following May, and to lay hold of some important related facts.

To begin with it should be clear, and it is worth repeating, that no matter what "Treaty" came from London it was likely to divide Dail Eireann - a broad spectrum of political opinion

---

[74] It included Lloyd George, Winston Churchill, Austen Chamberlain and Lord Birkenhead - F. E. Smith.

[75] See Dorothy Macardle, *The Irish Republic*; the author's *Birth of A Republic* and *The Civil War in Ireland* and other authorities.

united primarily on the common platform of national self-determination - into Government and Opposition parties.

The main contentious aspects of the Treaty itself were:

1/ Rejection by the British of Republic status;

2/ an Oath of Allegiance to the British monarch from public representatives, meaning the Irish would remain British subjects, not free citizens;

3/ Northern Ireland – removed from the agenda under informal British assurances that a Boundary Commission would determine a statelet of four counties which would be economically non-viable and would thus be compelled to unite with the rest of Ireland. (The outclassed Irish delegation - and the Dail Cabinet – appear to have accepted at face value these absurd opportunistic assurances purporting – of all things - to minimise Britain's primary strategic interest).

Matters were further compounded by the British who held that the Executives established under Government of Ireland Act, namely the Governments of Northern Ireland (more or less active) and of Southern Ireland (moribund), should administer the new agreement – the Treaty.

But, of course, it was not to be that simple. The agreement would have no smooth passage in Ireland.

The Treaty divided the country from top to bottom. The Cabinet and, some weeks later, uni-party Dail Eireann split on the issue. After a long and anguished debate in which the essence and spirit of the unity that had brought them to where they were no less than the divisions that now tormented them, were laid bare, Dail Eireann approved the Treaty by a slender majority of seven votes on January 7th 1922.

The question then arose as to what body would administer until a government of the new state – the Irish Free State – was elected. Except in British law the so-called Southern Government of Ireland did not exist. Divided Dail Eireann could not administer an instrument the main purpose of which was its own disestablishment.

It is possible, had the Dail Cabinet accepted the agreement and had the Dail reconstituted itself that the question might

163

have been resolved. But that did not happen. Dail Eireann was a republican parliament for all Ireland and under its existing constitution, could not do that. Another formula was required.

Consequently, following that critical vote, Dail deputies who had supported the Treaty voted into existence a provisional government of which Michael Collins, the dominant figure of the Treaty negotiations, was chairman. The question of whether or not it had a mandate from the people was vexed[76]. Its function was to introduce and administer the provisions of the Treaty until an election took place in June and a constitution and government of the Irish Free State were promulgated.

The parliamentary situation in the country was then confused to the point of absurdity. Four separate executives existed, of which three – the Northern and Southern parliaments and the Provisional Government - were recognised by the British, while one was not. But the one that was not recognised by the British was the only one with a mandate from the Irish people.

The British found the establishment of the Provisional Government reassuring. That reassurance was reinforced when backing for the Treaty came from the Irish establishment in general, the Churches and most social and civic groups. But it was strengthened and encouraged most of all, perhaps, by the resuscitation and addition to this political crucible of another, and hitherto - on this issue – dormant, powerful ingredient, namely the Irish Parliamentary Party. Following its massive defeat in 1918 it had been effectively excluded from politics for more than three years. Now, minus title and separate identity, it flocked to support the Treaty, allied itself therewith and, firmly donning the treaty

---

[76] When asked about this, Ernest Blythe, said "In a crisis those with the power have the authority". Although known ever since as the "Provisional Government", the full title of this assembly was the "Provisional Government of the Irish Free State", the IFS being the name of the new state-to-be under the Treaty.

hat, took shelter beneath its umbrella. It brought with it the electoral and political apparatus that had been idle for more than three years - in some instances taking control of whither the umbrella was carried, how and by whom. It also brought with it encouragement and a honed tradition of political and parliamentary expertise. And so it was, in full-blooded support of the Treaty, that the IPP re-entered the political arena.

The administrative theory was that both the Provisional Government and Dail Eireann would operate in tandem until publication of the Constitution of the Irish Free State, the election took place and the new government took office to administer the terms of the Treaty[77]. An Opposition was anticipated from anti-Treaty and other deputies. Such was the theory.

The reality was somewhat different. In the seriously unsettled and turbulent circumstances that now began to torment the war-shaken nation, the differences between pro- and anti-Treaty adherents became a deep and emotional hair-trigger. The danger was that it could release military no less than constitutional conflict.

But to the British all this must have seemed a hugely satisfactory reason for self-congratulation. At last it looked as if the dangerous and troublesome republican element in Irish politics was sidelined and contained. And this time there would not, as in 1916, be failures of preparation and awareness. They first of all proceeded to take copper-fastening steps to see, irrespective of anything the Irish might do, that in fact the constitution of the new state would reflect the British interpretation of the Treaty to which it was subordinate. Secondly they determined to delay its publication until it was too late to 'adversely' affect voting patterns in the election.

---

[77] Because of the Northern administrations acceptance of the terms of the Government of Ireland Act the election was to be confined to the southern twenty-six counties only.

Having more or less correctly elicited the general mood in Ireland to be for peace, they then appear to have assumed, incorrectly, that this meant that republicanism was, if not defeated, at any rate no longer a factor so far as Britain's interests were concerned. They massively failed to take account of the fact that many on the treaty side, including Michael Collins, had, against their will and commitment, reluctantly accepted the Treaty as an imposition under threat, and remained convinced republicans. When, as it would, push came to shove, what would result from that?

After the establishment of the Provisional Government Dail deputies opposed to the Treaty found themselves in a quandary. They opposed the Provisional Government on all fronts, but mainly on the constitutional ground that one of its main functions was to disestablish Dail Eireann. Eamon de Valera was their political leader. After the vote that led to the establishment of the Provisional Government he resigned as President of the Dail and was succeeded by Arthur Griffith, a signatory of the Treaty and nominal leader of pro-Treaty supporters in Dail Eireann. He was not a member of the Provisional Government.

The dilemma of the anti-Treaty deputies was obvious. How, they asked, could they tell when the assembly functioned as Dail Eireann and when as the Provisional Government, which had no mandate from the people? They decided to attend the assembly only when it functioned unequivocally as Dail Eireann.

But this created a political vacuum for anti-Treaty supporters, the largest single bloc of whom was – critically - the Army now, again, become an independent body – a matter to be of great significance.

On the establishment of Dail Eireann in 1919 the Army Executive, until then a separate and autonomous body, placed itself as the army of the Republic under Dail authority, with the revived title Irish Republican Army[78].

After the creation of the Provisional Government it took a radical and far-reaching step, explained only by the highly charged circumstances. It revoked the 1919 decision accepting the authority of the Dail, resuming full authority and independent status with its own Executive. The move was not welcome to constitutionalists of either side. It meant that the Army, heightening the risk of (even local) armed hostilities, could act independently of political concerns and direction. In the event that is exactly what did happen on a nationwide scale. But not yet.

Further darkening the murky constitutional waters now beginning to overwhelm this feeble ship of state, and compounding the threat of military conflict, was the fact that the Provisional Government (in effect Collins himself) established another military force answerable only to it. From its base in Ballsbridge, Dublin, it became known as the Beggars' Bush force. At that time it consisted almost entirely of members of the Dublin Brigade loyal to Collins.

But there was now no military force that came under the control of Dail Eireann. Nor did the anti-Treaty deputies have the full allegiance of or authority over any military body. From this severe, sustained consequences would result a little later.

Of course the Army's difficulty was the same as that of everyone else; it, too, split on the issue of acceptance or non-acceptance of the Treaty; certain brigade and division areas became predominantly pro- or predominantly anti-Treaty, the large majority being anti-Treaty.

---

[78] After The Rising and – ironically enough – in British prison camps notably Frongoch and Reading Jail, the Volunteer structure was considerably reorganised with its connection to
the IRB more tacit. By 1919 many of its significant officers also held ranking positions in the IRB.

At times minor tensions spilled over into local conflict with the danger of these spreading. Fortunately, even in the most serious of such incidents – as in Limerick – wiser counsel prevailed. But not always to everyone's liking; Griffith was furious when a pleased Collins brought news of the settlement in Limerick.

Then occurred an event that was to have extreme, bizarre and disastrous consequences. A small group (the number varied slightly from time-to-time, but was normally plus or minus 120 people) of experienced, but extreme, militant republicans broke away from the revived, independent Army Executive on policy grounds. They occupied and fortified the home of the Irish judiciary and higher courts, the Four Courts building in Dublin. In rejecting the Army Executive they called on it, and on Dail Eireann, to reject the Treaty and, if necessary, face a resumption of war with Britain.

This concentrated convergence of crises brings us directly to the Collins/deValera Pact. After it was concluded in May the Four Courts garrison completely severed all connection with the Army Executive (although up to then it included twelve nominal members of it), rejected the Pact and declared itself an independent body whose aims and principles were those stated above which, they claimed, were also those of the Republic, to which they remained loyal. The Army Executive, on the other hand were prepared in principle to support the Pact.

That is an outline of the situation as it was when Collins and deValera hammered out the Pact and presented it to Dail Eireann and the country. The Pact proposed a programme to ease tensions and bring into office a coalition Sinn Fein government, the Third Dail. It would simultaneously implement the terms of the Treaty while pursuing a republican programme. The Collins/deValera Pact offered a constitutional, political and military solution, in essence taking the view that the Treaty was not written on stone tablets and did not prevent constitutional progress towards achieving full national sovereignty.

168

It proposed that both sides in Sinn Fein, pro- and anti-Treaty shades of opinion, would nominate a joint panel of Sinn Fein candidates in the forthcoming election, sixty-six from pro-Treaty supporters and fifty-eight from the others "without prejudice to their present respective positions". Those elected would form the coalition government, which would be the third Dail Eireann. The election was scheduled for three weeks away. In the meantime the Constitution was due to be published. Though the Pact offered a constitutional way forward it was clearly an unusual political solution. Nor was it all plain sailing. Collins was well aware that not all – or indeed a majority – of the members of the Provisional Government, of which he was Chairman, were happy with the Pact (ministries, of course, being at stake), and Griffith, President of Dail Eireann, was bitterly opposed to it.

It had also been agreed that the forthcoming election would not be held on the issue of the Treaty, but, in the interests of peace, in order to create the National Coalition Government.

The proposed cabinet was to consist of five pro-Treaty members and, very likely given their majority, the President; and four anti-Treaty members and, for similar reasons, the Minister for Defence (to be elected by the Army). But the most important point of all was that the appalling vista of civil war had been averted. Or had it?

Reactions
Between 1916 and 1922 the Liberal, Lloyd George, headed a coalition government with a large and very hawkish Tory representation.

So far as Ireland was concerned British interest was what it had always been, strategic. Yet, while all things British undoubtedly remained best, the world had become an increasingly restless place where long established certainties were not always perceived as the unquestioned verities they used to be.

Containment in Ireland, the threatened back-door, was therefore, necessary. The Treaty question being settled more or less satisfactorily with Britain retaining for as long as it was possible to anticipate its strategic presence in Northern Ireland, it indeed began to look as if British interests would be satisfactorily served. If that led to trouble, and trouble there was to be, let it be resolved by the Irish themselves in whatever way they chose, so long – that is - as it suited British interests.

Anxious to guide events in Ireland as best they could to their advantage, they found the formation of the Provisional Government encouraging. It clearly seemed to indicate plain sailing for the introduction of a constitution and government subordinate to their interpretation of the Treaty terms.

As tensions in Ireland between the pro- and anti-Treaty factions continued, once or twice almost boiling over into an all-out shooting war, it did indeed begin to seem as if it would be only a matter of time before the uneasy peace, fluttering like some tattered and ephemeral shawl from the troubled shoulders of Dark Rosaleen, was finally ripped away by internecine strife. With a polished air of I-told-you-so the British happily distanced themselves from this distressing outcome of the Treaty. That is until the Pact was announced.

It outraged the British. They claimed the Pact to be a breach of the Treaty. They feared – probably correctly – that an elected government in Ireland composed of a reunited Sinn Fein led by either Collins or deValera, but certainly with both in cabinet, would, while complying with the letter of the Treaty, work towards a fulfilment of the republican programme; that it could target Northern Ireland, then in a state of violent and bloody turmoil; and, worst of all, that it would threaten their particular interests.

At any cost they must retain their essential foothold in Ireland. The British GOC in Ireland, General Sir Nevil Macready, was promptly ordered to prepare for a bombardment of Dublin, while the military commander in

Dublin, Maj. Gen. George Boyd, was ordered to halt repatriation of British troops and to reoccupy the city in the event of a coalition Sinn Fein government taking office. Plans for a naval blockade and to re-occupy the country were also considered[79]. Finally great pressure was applied on Collins to renounce the Pact that Britain claimed was a breach of the Treaty.

The constitution of the new Irish Free State had not been published. There had, as in the Treaty negotiations, been protracted discussions on it, each side determined to achieve the result most favourable to itself. Collins's instructions to the Irish committee were to produce "an independent Irish constitution that would mention neither the British Crown nor the Anglo-Irish Treaty. The purpose was to prevent an Irish civil war by reconciling most of the anti-treaty leaders to the Free State"[80]. To no avail. The Irish committee produced three drafts, but none was acceptable to London.

Now, in addition to the above military dispositions the British dug their heels in regarding the constitution. It was more vital than ever to ensure that their version resulted. Publication must be delayed for as long as possible in order to minimise any risk of adverse reaction to it from anti-Treaty voters and *quondam* pro-Treaty supporters alike, before the election.

So far, so good.

The election took place on June 16th. The constitution was published only that morning. British percipience and strategy seemed justified. The election results (on June 24th) were closer than comfortable and, had it not been for that strategy, might have been even closer. While the results favoured the Treaty, a substantial minority still opposed it.

British reaction both to the Constitution and, by linkage, to the election was summarised: "Instead of weakening the

---

[79] Whether Britain had at that time the manpower to take and hold a militarily resistant Ireland is, as we shall see, questionable.

[80] *The Irish Civil War and the Drafting of the Free State Constitution* – D. H. Akenson and J. F. Fallin, Minnesota, 1970.

Treaty, as was generally expected in Ireland, it underwrites the Treaty and underscores the Treaty in a most emphatic manner. The English victory is plain"[81].

Even at this remove it is not easy to fully grasp the hows and whys of the Irish authorities, having worked so intensely – and with good reason - for a different outcome, agreeing to the British version of the constitution.

It is no harm to summarise again:-

1. Following The Rising the people, in 1918, committed themselves through the ballot-box to re-acquiring self-determination with a native government. Dail Eireann was established in 1919 and the War of Independence began the same year.

2. After more than two years of war and (proscribed) Irish governance a truce was declared in July, 1921. This was followed by negotiations leading to formal discussions for an Agreement between the peoples of Ireland and Great Britain. These began on 11th October and ended on 6th December, 1921.

3. Throughout, the British refused to acknowledge or to consider any question of a republic, or that the Irish delegates represented or had been appointed by Dail Eireann, which they also refused to acknowledge, taking the view that they were in discussion with representatives of the (Southern) Irish parliament deriving authority under the Government of Ireland Act. Representatives of the Northern government absented themselves from the negotiations.

4. The Treaty split the Irish people from top to bottom. The Treaty proved unacceptable to a majority in the Army.

5. A provisional government was formed by the majority (by seven) of pro-Treaty deputies. Michael Collins was its chairman. Its purpose was to introduce the terms of the Treaty prior to an election in June to be followed by the formation of a government of the new state-to-be,

---

[81] *Sunday Times*, June 18, 1922.

The Irish Free State. One effect would be that Dail Eireann would simultaneously be disestablished.

6. By March all this had raised tension in the country to the point where civil war seemed possible.

7. In May Collins and deValera, respectively Chairman of the Provisional Government and former President of Dail Eireann, then political leader of anti-Treaty Sinn Fein, produced an agreed peace formula, the main proposal of which was that a Coalition Sinn Fein Government – the Third Dail - be formed after the forthcoming election. This was the Collins/deValera Pact.

8. The British were infuriated by this, claiming it to be a breach of the Treaty. They ordered repatriation of British troops in Ireland halted, their GOC there to prepare to bombard the city in the event of the coalition republican government taking office and to prepare plans for the reoccupation of the country. Collins came under intense pressure from them to reject the Pact.

9. The election was held on the same day as the terms of the new constitution were published.

Of these points 3, 7, 8 and 9 are the most important in our context.

The underlying British fear of and hostility to republicanism of any sort, especially an Irish variety, which they had rejected from the outset, is abundantly evident throughout this period.

While Collins and deValera were both deeply committed to the Pact and its terms, neither man had the full support of those he represented. Not all – even most – of the pro-Treaty leaders approved, while the Army Executive, with allegiance only to the Republic, looked askance at deValera. But both men were confident of carrying their respective majorities.

Nonetheless, in spite of the Pact and that confidence, civil war exploded 39 days later, scarring the nation and the body politic of the neophyte state, physically and morally, for generations to come. What had happened?

At precisely the point when tensions between Britain and Ireland and between Irish partisans of one side or another were at their highest, and the Pact or war - which is what it came down to – was the boiling issue, all was profoundly worsened in a totally unforeseen manner.

As if it fell, like some astounding, pivotal and unsuspected profundity of Greek tragedy to transform plot and setting from one of impending, but uncertain, menace, to one of stark and inevitable disaster, a totally unforeseen event in London brought the entire situation to the point where the full horror of war – in one form or another – seemed inescapable.

On June 22nd, a week to the day following the election and the publication of the Irish Free State Constitution, that notorious anti-Irish Irishman, former Chief of the Imperial General Staff, General Sir Henry Wilson, who, in March, had been appointed military advisor to the Northern Government by its prime minister Sir James Craig, was murdered on his doorstep in London by two Irishmen who – though former members of the British Army (one of them had lost a leg at Ypres) - were IRA Volunteers. It could not have happened at a worse time for the Irish. Collins in particular found himself in an extraordinary dilemma[82]. British outrage intensified.

For reasons that remain unclear, and in spite of the fact that the Four Courts garrison issued a statement declaring

---

[82] Illustrating the complex cross-currents of loyalty and conflict ravaging the hearts and minds of the people, most of all, perhaps, those in Sinn Fein, is the fact that Sean MacBride then in a position both anomalous and far from uncommon when, although a member of the Four Courts garrison, he was procuring arms for Michael Collins for shipment to the Northern brigades, told the author in 1987 that he was satisfied that the order for Wilson's shooting came from Collins. The probability is that the order had been issued some time previously and, following the Truce, that it was assumed to have been rescinded – an assumption not clarified to the Volunteers on the spot.

that "the shooting of Sir Henry Wilson was not done at the instance of the Irish Republican Army", the British decided that the order to kill Wilson had issued from there. To this day it is not known if this was simply misjudgement – attributing to the tiny Four Courts garrison influence they did not have (as, in 1916, they attributed imaginary power and influence to Roger Casement) – or if it were used as a convenient *casus belli* in Ireland. The immediate reaction was to summon General Macready to London.

There he was ordered to attack the Four Courts as soon as possible. He returned to Dublin to prepare to carry out his orders, but with some reluctance since he did not believe that it would be possible to hold Ireland with less than 200,000 fresh troops which did not exist. But then Lloyd George had a better idea. Within twenty-four hours of being issued Macready's orders were cancelled. Lloyd George then summoned Collins to London.

In keeping with British post-Treaty Irish policy being as intelligently self-interested as their pre-Truce policy had been foolish and counter-productive, Lloyd George, having successfully diluted the Free State Constitution and unbalanced the Pact, now found to his hand the perfect lever to precipitate an attack on the Four Courts – but not by the British. The reasons for this proposed attack, flying as they do in the face of reason and logic so far as the Four Courts are concerned, are not hard to find. For Lloyd Gorge here was a golden opportunity to block any question of a republican coalition government in Ireland and to secure the Treaty on British terms. More importantly it would have immense beneficial political fall-out and would do so without cost in British lives or to the Exchequer.

So he brought pressure on Collins to attack the Four Courts with the Beggars' Bush force on behalf of the Provisional Government. The alternative he proposed was precisely the ultimatum he had issued at the end of the Treaty negotiations. If Collins didn't settle with the Four Courts 'die-hards' and put an end to their disruptive and murderous activities, the British would do so themselves. In that event the Irish people must face all the resulting (unspecified) consequences[83].

Lloyd George's purpose is clear; if, as he seemed to believe in spite of the contrary evidence, the Four Courts garrison represented the core leadership of anti-Treaty support and had – as he may in fact have believed – also been responsible for killing Wilson and other hostile acts, eliminating them would, by smashing it before it got started, be the best way of achieving the desirable outcome of preventing the coalition republican government from taking office. It would ensure containment, even elimination, of the republican element - as had, mistakenly, seemed to be the case with the establishment of the Provisional Government. Lastly, and perhaps most brilliantly, he would pressurise Collins into doing all this for him.

If the possibility of this resulting in civil war in Ireland occurred to him it was unlikely to have been a cause of much concern. The bottom line for Lloyd George must have been that if civil war resulted in Ireland that would be infinitely preferable to any stressful, uncertain – and expensive - involvement by Britain and would, whatever the outcome, further weaken Irish resistance to the British view of the Treaty and would achieve British objectives with no direct British involvement; a happy resolution.

But this design was flawed in a number of respects. Better informed than Lloyd George, Collins's view of things would have been quite different and need not, and probably did not, include abandoning either the Pact or the republican coalition. Since this goes against long established popular opinion, and since herein lies the key that unlocks and throws

---

[83] However, given world and British public opinion alone, the likelihood of Britain taking such action seems doubtful. British military action on such a scale in Ireland would undoubtedly have led to a resumption of war requiring, as Macready said, 200,000 fresh troops they did not have. In all probability it was an idle threat of brinkmanship. However it worked.

open to scrutiny the evasions of our third myth, an outline of how this conclusion may be reached is important.

Dilemma

Collins's had a twofold dilemma. Firstly he was under heavy pressure from the British because of the Pact. Secondly, he was threatened with the formidable choice either of attacking the Four Courts himself, or – as he was led to believe – have the British do so, and face resumption of war and another onslaught by the British Army on the country, which would certainly result from such an attack by them.

Far from being a man to crumple under pressure, no less was he one to fail to see and to press advantages. Certainly the current situation presented a monstrous dilemma, in many ways as great as that of the Treaty itself. Matters were close to being beyond control - but not yet. No one knew better than Collins the reality about the Four Courts. He, more than anyone, knew the truth about Wilson's murder. He was in a unique position to judge how matters stood in Ireland regarding the balance of political and military power. Above all he understood what the Pact and the proposed coalition that he planned with de Valera could achieve for the people and the country.

The pragmatic republican, Collins knew that there was only a tiny, dissident group opposed to everything - the Treaty, the Pact and the Army Executive - to deal with in the Four Courts. He was actively working with them on a day-to-day basis to supply weapons to Northern IRA units. Since the Four Courts dissidents had rejected the Army Executive it followed that there was no likelihood of intervention from that quarter were he to apply pressure on them.

And there were two reasons why pressure was required. The first, of course, was the British ultimatum. Even though it was initially evidently based on misinformation, by that stage Lloyd George must at least have known what Collins's

177

general views on the Four Courts were. If so – and it is inconceivable that it was otherwise – it did not affect matters so far as he was concerned. His ultimatum stood. The second reason, from Collins's point of view, was even more important and was typical of his thinking. Pressure on the Four Courts would not only reassure the British, it would also offset the prospect of action by them that might rekindle the war. To deal with the Four Courts, act of expediency though it might be, could also result in the British playing into his hands. He was well aware of that. Anti-Treaty military leadership lay with the Army Executive and its political leadership with deValera. The small group of extreme, dissident and doctrinaire republicans comprising the Four Courts garrison had little power or influence.

While other than their opposition to the Treaty, there was little relationship between them both had in principle accepted the Pact that the Four Courts garrison had rejected outright (as had some of the pro-Treaty leaders both in Dail Eireann and in the Provisional Government) and were willing to give it a chance. If we are to believe MacBride he knew without doubt that the trigger that brought British wrath to this pitch, namely the killing of Wilson, had nothing whatever to do with the Four Courts.

Like a safe haven glimpsed through a shifting mist by the captain of an imperilled ship, Collins can not but have seen in subduing the Four Courts garrison the glimmering prospect of a secure resolution to his woeful dilemma. It would simultaneously and satisfactorily enable him to comply with British demands, while at the same time proceeding with the terms of the Pact – a bold, electrifying and typical Collins idea.

The small garrison would be called on to surrender; might be expected to put up token resistance - no more, and then surrender. In that event the situation was resolved - but not on Lloyd George's terms. It would not result in internecine turmoil. Quite the opposite.

With the difficulty of the Four Courts out of the way and following a period of restoring calm and of convincing his pro-Treaty colleagues, the sovereign, elected, coalition republican government of Ireland might then proceed as planned without further foreseeable threat from Britain.

From such a perspective it could well seem that by taking British intervention out of the equation Lloyd George might unwittingly have played into Collins's hands.

There are weaknesses as well as possibilities in this estimate. The major weakness would appear to lie in a speech by Collins in Cork on June 14th, two days before the election in which he seems to go back on the coalition proposal when he said: - "I am not hampered now by being on a platform where there are coalitionists. I can make a straight appeal to you – to vote for the candidate you think best of, whom the electors of Cork think will carry on best in the future the work they want carried on ..."

The speech has generally been taken to be an outright repudiation of the Pact and the proposed coalition. But is it? It is certainly much less clear-cut and not as downright specific as he might have been when, were such his intention, there was no reason not to be blunt. Another, and, in the above context perhaps more correct, reading of it suggests a more plausible intention, that is that the sentences are the equivocal words of a master political craftsman addressing his own electorate in his own constituency.

Collins had again been to London, on 12th, meeting Lloyd George, and Churchill on the 13th, the day before he made this speech, returning to Ireland overnight. These facts put the speech in a context that gives the above outline considerable validity. In this ambiguous rallying call, rather than its being an outright rejection of the Pact proposals, Collins can be seen working to keep both the British and the electorate reassured. Moreover, the constitution – the adverse terms of which he is almost certain to have known at that stage – had not yet been published. And, of course, the fact that he was speaking to his own electorate in his own constituency is also a point of considerable significance.

All-in-all, with two days to go to the election and publication of the unfavourable constitution, the probability is that the devious Collins was, as ever, publicly playing both ends against the middle in order to achieve his purpose[84].

Two day before the coalition Third Dail was due to assemble on June 30th and ten days after the election, following a surrender demand, the Four Courts was attacked at 0405 in the morning of June 28th.

It is far too easy, with well-developed hindsight, to criticise dedicated and earnest people gripped in the vice of time. Time and partisanship all too often convert those great toilers who hammered on the anvils of history from beings, like the rests of us, afflicted with doubts and shortcomings, into superhuman and persuasive images of ideals. But that is a misleading semblance; wishful thinking that only makes it all the more difficult to judge the reality. Indeed we have clearly seen this process at work in our own time in an immediate manner that, thanks to virtually instant and universal communications, would have been impossible a few short

---

[84] Sean MacBride gave the author a detailed account of his meeting with Collins on the subject of sending arms to the northern brigades on the day before the shelling of the Four Courts.
In "Intelligence report on the 2nd Northern Division as it stood in 1922", undated, General (then Major) Dan McKenna (Army Chief-of-Staff during and after the Emergency, 1939-45) included: -
"(2) After the Treaty was signed, the late General Collins who was then Chairman of the Provisional Government, and the mouthpiece of the new order of things, impressed strongly on the Nationalists of the Six Counties that, although the Treaty might have *an outward expression of Partition*, the Government had plans whereby they would make it impossible, and that Partition would never be recognised even though it might mean the smashing of the Treaty (author's italics)".
And, of course Collins's speech was made before Wilson was killed. But the issues were there before that. His murder simply exacerbated them and seemed to give Lloyd George some additional leverage.

decades ago. In such circumstances as those that obtained between the Pact and the civil war uncertainty is heavily charged with emotion. Who, given that jumble of partisan-sculpted alleged facts still infesting some accounts of it, can uncritically and with certainty point the finger at right and wrong?

Once the British presented Collins with the unyielding and compelling choice of either subduing the Four Courts or a resumption of war, Collins really had only one troublesome option. It can be, and it is, argued that Collins should have outfaced the British.

So far as he was aware to have done so could have meant a resumption of war. He could not have known how weak British military resources were at that stage or that it was extremely unlikely that they could have carried out their threat.

Nothing in any of this suggests that his own republicanism was diminished. On the contrary. But there remains the considerable paradox that he, Chairman of the Provisional Government that included in its brief the disestablishment of Dail Eireann, was at constant loggerheads with Griffith, the President of Dail Eireann, on the question of resolving confrontations between pro- and anti-Treaty forces. More than once Griffith expressed the view, shared by some other cabinet colleagues, that matters should be brought to a head and be over and done with. Collins, on the other hand, is on record as stating that he'd like to "continue now and finish the fight" (against Britain) and that he felt closer to anti-Treatyites than to his pro-Treaty colleagues[85]. "Collins told the Dail that the Pact was more important to him than the Treaty"[86].

In all of this the power and influence of the IRB, which remained active throughout, must not be overlooked. Many of the leading figures involved on all sides were members of

---

[85] "I am in sympathy with a majority of the IRA. I wish to continue now and finish the fight...." Letter to Paddy Daly in April.
[86] Michael Farrell, *The Irish Times*, 15 December, 1982.

the IRB. Liam Lynch, for instance, attended many IRB meetings during this period which were also attended by Collins and members from the Four Courts.

Griffith was a continuing problem so far as Collins and his intentions were concerned. The sometime pacifist Griffith had seen his non-violent creation, Sinn Fein, become increasingly militaristic. His high-minded and idiosyncratic sense of honour had been strikingly and unhappily demonstrated during the Treaty negotiations[87]. His behaviour and attitude from the moment the Treaty was signed seem to indicate that, having done so, that same sense of wayward and dogmatic honour brought him to being not just the strongest advocate of the Treaty, but also of bringing matters to a head with those opposed to it whatever the consequences. His fury in March when Collins defused the serious confrontation in Limerick was matched by his reaction to the Pact.

As we have judged, Collins foresaw a solution – if a difficult one – in the national interest that must surely, using minimum and restricted force, have seemed possible. Here was no Mexican stand-off between two sides of the entire Army. The problem was a tiny – at best perhaps 160 or so – group of extremists on their own without political or other backing. Contain them - and full steam ahead. The British demands would be satisfied, even wrong-footed and, thus, the danger of their attacking Dublin and precipitating war would be eliminated, or at least minimised, and any threat of civil war set aside. Most important of all – if from the British viewpoint hugely equivocal – the new Third Dail would take office and implement its dual programme of administering under the Treaty while following a republican programme.

---

[87] Notably when he gave a letter of undertaking to Lloyd George assuring him that the Irish were prepared to agree to conditions which L. G. requested in advance in order to enable L.G. to offset an anticipated attack from the National Unionist Conference and survive a vote of censure in the House of Commons.

But, by 0200 on the fatal morning of June 28th, things had completely altered. The situation that might have made all this possible no longer existed. A matter of mere hours before the attack on the Four Courts and unknown to Collins, at about 01.00, the grave differences between the Four Courts dissidents and the Army Executive had been resolved. The Four Courts garrison had recanted and had again accepted Executive authority – including, significantly, their attitude to the proposed coalition. But this also meant that an attack on either would constitute an attack on both.

Civil War

The immediate question must be:- What if Collins had known of the reconciliation between the Executive and the Four Courts? Would the attack still have gone ahead? Logic says that it would not. There are other, very powerful indications suggesting the same conclusion.

To believe that Collins, had he known full-scale civil war must ensue, would in the final critical hour have attacked the Four Courts is unthinkable and uncharacteristic.

Taking account of his known views, of what he had stated publicly, and that the Beggars' Bush force came under his direct control, it is legitimate to speculate that, had he known the changed and more unified circumstances, instead of attacking the Four Courts and precipitating nation-wide civil war, he might well have decided not to do so and risk outfacing the British.

And there were other options. Given his close involvement and cooperation with the Four Courts right up to that point and their mutual membership of the IRB, it is not beyond the bounds of possibility that Collins would have come to an agreement with the powerful Army Executive.

Of course this is conjectural, leaving it open to the possibility of being dismissed as excessively speculative and inconclusive – were it not for one other extremely significant fact.

183

The chronology, logic and pattern of events up to this are now reasonably clear. But at precisely this point there is a large and surprising hole.

For some reason a significant and illuminating event at this crucial juncture has been treated merely as an unimportant and isolated occurrence, disregarded, and been all but written out of the history books. Given the lingering prevalence of partisan opinion, this, in an odd way, helps reinforce its importance.

As we know the views of those committed, more or less unequivocally, to the Treaty quite often reject any question of an alternative to the simplistic view that Collins decided to smash the Pact, the Coalition Government and the republican opposition in the Four Courts, in that order. These views also reject the idea that he was looking for a way to end hostilities, rather than an unconditional defeat of the anti-Treatyites in the field of battle.

But the facts indicate otherwise. If one were to subscribe to the view that Collins unquestioningly intended to carry out the terms of the British ultimatum such views do have a certain trite logic; but neither do they make sense. Collins was the originator of the Pact. He had, in his own words, already, once, experienced the affliction of "the duress of the facts"[88] at the hands of the British and was unlikely to want a repetition. Taking his well-demonstrated and articulated attitude into account, both before and after the outbreak of civil war, these superficial views tend to wither.

Here some other relevant points must be considered, not least the fact that Collins was Head Centre – that is Chairman – of the IRB and, in accordance with the two decisions taken by the IRB Council in 1873, therefore the provisional President of Ireland until such time as the people voted for another. Should the time-factor be thought to render this irrelevant it might be noted that the first of these decisions –

---

[88] Collins's description of the *force majeure* under which he signed the Treaty.

184

namely that the IRB Council would act as the Government of Ireland until, etc., - was rescinded with the establishment of Dail Eireann on the proposal of General Sean MacEoin acting on Collins's behalf in 1919. But, since a president of Ireland had not been elected, the other decision still stood.

It follows that Collins, and many of the IRB, saw Collins in that capacity rather than – or as well as – that of Chairman of the Provisional Government.

There is the further fact that, while Griffith had been the nominal leader of the Irish delegation to the Treaty negotiations, the *de facto* role of leader quickly passed to Collins (due, in part, to Griffith's state of health). Now, Chairman of the Provisional Government, Collins again seemed to be taking precedence over Griffith, President of Dail Eireann. Whether this, and/or the question of subsequent leadership, may have contributed to some of the tension between Griffith and Collins then and later is hard to say.

Significantly, too, Collins, the avowed republican, was surrounded and frequently challenged by pro-Treaty colleagues with whom he had little in common - in particular when he strove for an accommodation acceptable to both sides – as in the Pact and in his subsequent endeavours to "bring this thing to an end" (the civil war).

Regarding the immediate crisis in June 1922 of "dealing with" the Four Courts, these factors help put the reality into perspective.

And so to the side-lined event of cardinal significance at that point. As soon as the attack on the Four Courts took place Liam Lynch, Chief of Staff of the Army Executive - with which the Four Courts garrison had been reconciled just before the attack and whose authority it again acknowledged – immediately decided to return to Munster, the base of his 1st, Division, the largest and strongest in the Army. With some of his staff he set out from his Clarence Hotel headquarters that morning to take the train to Cork from Kingsbridge (Heuston) Station.

He had prepared a statement for issue to the Press. For obvious reasons there had as yet not been time to publish it. In part it read: "... we appeal to all citizens who have withstood unflinchingly the oppression of the enemy during the past six years, to rally to the support of the Republic and recognise that the *resistance now being offered* is but the continuance of the struggle that was suspended by the truce with the British. We especially appeal to our former comrades in the Irish Republic ..."

En route to the station Lynch and his companions were stopped by Beggars' Bush troops and arrested. Brought for interrogation they were soon afterwards released in time to catch the train. This, it may be reasoned, was on the orders of Collins, no other officer having authority to release the Army Chief-of-Staff and GOC the 1st Division once he had been detained.

Two things are clear. Collins did not know of Lynch's call to arms and he still expected that whatever conflict there might be would be limited to the Four Courts. This reinforces the view that his purpose at that point was to bring order to the very volatile situation, prevent a resumption of war with Britain, and, one must assume, to work, towards the republic to which he was committed. Unknown to him, the context had changed.

What difference it might have made had Collins known of the reconciliation between the Army Executive and the Four Courts garrison before the attack remains speculative. But the core fact is that several hours after the attack began, Liam Lynch, the Army Chief-of-Staff and GOC of the most powerful, influential and successful division in the army, together with his commanders, aides and staff, having been arrested and detained, were released to continue their journey south to their headquarters and base.

To believe that Lynch, his staff and some of the commanders of the largest and most powerful division in the Army, known to be avowedly anti-Treaty, would have been released had Collins believed (i) that civil war was imminent,

186

(ii) that Lynch intended to put that division in the field against him, is ridiculous. It is clear, therefore, that Collins neither anticipated nor intended nationwide civil war to result from the attack on the Four Courts. Equally clearly he could not have known that the Four Courts garrison was again under Lynch's command.

Collins could not have suspected that Lynch was returning to Cork in order to take command of an Army he considered to have been attacked by Collins's troops, nor could he have anticipated that the outcome of allowing Lynch to continue his journey would be full-scale civil war.

The release of Lynch fills the blank in the question.

While it is evident that Collins's intention was to contain the Four Courts 'situation' with minimum force, the changed and unforeseen circumstances that led to the spread of the conflict to the rest of the Army and country created an altogether different and unwelcome situation for which he was completely unprepared. He would neither have wanted such an outcome, nor was he ready for it. For one thing the troops at the disposal of the Army Executive outnumbered the Beggars' Bush force by about three to one at that stage. Though he did not yet know this, whatever hope Collins might have entertained of there being only the small Four Courts garrison to deal with was gone. Ironically the event that brought this calamity about also, had he but known it, resolved his problem regarding the Four Courts situation. By coming again under the control of the Army Executive, which accepted a wait-and-see attitude towards the Pact, the Four Courts garrison had resolved that problem for Collins. It is true that – but again with brilliant hindsight – some of the Four Courts garrison attributed the reconciliation to the publication, and their joint rejection, of the constitution. But that had been two weeks earlier and can hardly have been the basis.

There is no doubt that Civil War was avoidable. It solved nothing that could not have been solved peaceably. It is therefore all the more regrettable that the Pact, which could have prevented it and brought constitutional accord, has been ignored. But, ignored or not, it remains crucial to any understanding of how and why the Civil War began; how and why later political alignments developed and, to some extent, how and why Sinn Fein and the IRA were later to become established as political sub cultures in a sovereign Irish society. And then cast aside the mantle of the moral high ground that had served them so well and adopted – or tried to – wanton terrorism and attempted to make of it a legitimate tactic of freedom and resistance.

If I may end with a quote from one of my books dealing with the period:-

"The time is long overdue when the divisive issues of the Treaty and the civil war were put into perspective. Here is no right and wrong (though one must exclude some individual acts which occurred in the course of events). To believe otherwise is to believe that the honourable were dishonourable, that the dedicated were unpatriotic and that those who had fought as companions-in-arms for justice and liberty were no more than time-serving opportunists" - *Birth of A Republic*, p. 275.

A CONSIDERATION

What If Collins
Were Not Killed?

A CONSIDERATION

What If Collins Were not Killed?

THE ABOVE QUESTION is often responded to by proponents of one side or the other in the civil war conflict with fervid partisanship. It deserves better. The question must turn a spotlight on the events of August, 1922 and, hopefully, reveal true, and hitherto obscured, historical data.

Though adrift on the shapeless tides of mixed prejudice and fact, the question nevertheless is one of the most important unanswered – if speculative – considerations of that period for, conjecture notwithstanding, there is no doubt that the life or death of this one man profoundly affected – not just the duration and outcome of the war – but how it was conducted, and its aftermath.

As with so much else from the 1910-1923 formative period of Irish history misunderstanding and confusion often obscure fact – further compounded by today's witless phoney-liberal requirement for tolerance at any price to the point of discarding dignity and identity, principle and probity[89].

The previous essay suggests that Collins did not anticipate full-scale civil war to result from the attack on the Four Courts.

The extraordinary pressure being exerted on him by the British, and its purpose – to smash the Pact and prevent any possibility of a republican Dail/programme re-emerging – and Collins's response; the complex inter- and cross relationships affecting members of Sinn Fein, the Volunteers, the IRB have been outlined.

Collins was actively providing arms to the Army in the Northern statelet with a view to continuing activities there. He'd reached the Pact agreement with de Valera for coalition of all shades of opinion (except the small group in the Four Courts) with the Third Dail. The inaugural meeting of that parliament was prorogued due to the outbreak of hostilities - in other words meetings were discontinued for a time without dissolving, in this case until September. Accordingly that proposed Third Dail could still be held to be the elected assembly under the Pact. Following the unexpected spread of the conflict there are clear indications that Collins's intention was to end the fighting as soon as possible. Moreover he was the only man in the country at the time capable of making that happen.

Those enticed by cognitive historical convenience-food and relishing what they'd prefer to have had happen rather than what actually occurred would do well to remember that the Ireland Collins lived and worked in was very different to the Ireland of today. To distort the past and the lives and responsibilities of the people in it by expecting them to have behaved according to a level of idealism that we ourselves have not achieved, is plain ludicrous.

---

[89] The attempt (Irish Times 21st June, 2006) by Mr. Bouchier Hayes to whitewash the Black and Tans and Auxiliaries and the preposterous and shameful erection of a monument to the murderous Francis Drake being two examples of such fawning.

The times differed in many ways - the number of road vehicles, non-existence of super-markets, minimal cost air-travel, and so on, are not meant to be examples. Two major lifestyles, neither of them demonstrating social or technological comparison with today, were the norm. These were, respectively, the rural and urban lifestyles, or ways of life, of which the former was by far the more dominant and widespread. Moreover, social revolution and genuine liberal thought and teaching notwithstanding, both were deeply conservative. To judge from his writings, even from a revolutionary – or rather republican – viewpoint and conviction, Collins himself was conservative in outlook.

It may be taken, therefore, that he brought these values with him in trying to resolve the civil war debacle. We may also reasonably infer from what is set out below that his urgent intention was to end hostilities and inaugurate the new parliament under the agreed procedures.

While there is nothing to even suggest that Collins wanted the war to continue to a victory or defeat conclusion, the indicators all point to the fact that he wanted – and was endeavouring – to end it, even in the face of hostility and criticism from his own side. His earlier efforts for reconciliation brought criticism from some of his own colleagues in both the Second Dail (notably Griffith, and O'Higgins and Ernest Blythe) and the Provisional government - that had endured and, in some cases, hardened. It should be remembered that, acknowledged or not, post-war political power was now a very clear issue and motive. Moreover the IPP rump, excluded for four years from direct involvement in Irish politics, now brought all its experience and political expertise to bear in support of the Treaty faction.

Collins's visit to (republican) Brigadier Tom Malone in Portlaoise prison on his way south to the fateful tour of Cork and his comment at the time to the then Lieutenant, soon to be Colonel and later Lieut-General in the established Irish Defence Forces, M. J. Costelloe, that 'The three Toms will

192

end this', is another indication of his anxiety to end hostilities (less than two months after the attack on the Four Courts). The other two Toms were Brigadier Tom Barry, then in Kilmainham jail, and Tom Hales, brigadier of the Third Cork Brigade and who, ironically, and perhaps significantly, was the officer in command of the area where the Beal na mBlath ambush took place. Sean Hales, his brother and a brigadier with the pro-Treaty forces, had been sent by Collins to contact Tom. The significant and generally overlooked point is that, after being mysteriously absent for some hours, Tom Hales returned to the ambush site and without reference to his superior officers ordered the ambush to be stood down[90]. Six men were left behind to clear the mine and barricade and to provide cover. By a chance of Fate and war Collins's convoy came on the scene while the retiring ambush party was ahead of it on the road. The clearing party fired a warning shot to alert them and so precipitated the action at Beal na mBlath in which Collins was killed. Whether Tom Hales's action was a result of his having been contacted by his brother, Sean, and alerted to the IRB meeting that night in Cork, is now beyond determination.

Collins' remark to the young Costello that; "The three Toms will end this –" meaning Barry, Malone and Hales, has no meaning unless taken in the context of his anxiety to end the war. He knew that these three men, two of them also IRB men, had the power to influence huge numbers of anti-Treaty forces – still in a state of incomplete mobilisation - no less than many if not all of the Army Executive. It should also be seen in the context of Collins setting up the IRB meeting in Desmond's Hotel for the night of the 22nd, and, further, of sending Colonel Frank Thornton to contact Liam Deasy and de Valera. It should all be related to Tom Barry's statement

---

91 The questions that arise naturally are:- i/ Did Tom and Sean Hales meet as Collins had instructed the latter? If so, was Tom Hales aware of the proposed meeting that night in Desmond's Hotel, even if he weren't aware of it from IRB sources? He knew that Collins' route to Cork must lie through Beal na mBlath and is that why he stood down the ambush so as to avoid the danger of what precisely happened?

(to the author) regarding Collins conversation on the subject with himself: "Collins wanted to end it".

It will be noted that these steps taken by Collins were neither homogeneous nor part of a coordinated plan – also a strong indication that they formed no part of an overall design by Collins to continue the war into the future.

There can be little room for doubt as to what his intentions were when he left Dublin on Sunday, August 20th, *en route* for his inspection tour of Cork and Munster generally.

Finally what end would have been served at that stage for Collins by pursuing the war to a conclusion? There was the matter of his known policy on the North. He was, even then, in continuing contact with Northern units of all shades to whom he had already that week given an undertaking that they would not be compelled to take part in the fighting in the south.[91]

British imperial interests were what they had always been, strategic; enshrined in Lord Palmerston's dictum. (And it has not changed, except, like so much else, to have gone westward across the Atlantic in the 20th century).

In 1922, and for some 80 years afterwards, the British were determined at any cost to keep a foothold in Ireland. The Pact was a powerful threat to that strategic imperative. In the event they quite cynically encouraged the onset of civil war so that it would achieve what they wanted without their involvement.

Had Collins been successful in achieving a cessation of hostilities what, then, was the position? It would, in fact, have been a version of what he had been trying to achieve prior to the outbreak of the civil war, namely the elimination of the Four Courts garrison as a factor in the equation before the formation of the Third Dail.

His hand would, of course, have been strengthened, but there is no reason to believe that he would have wanted other

---

[91] At a meeting in Dublin. See footnote p. 180. Frank Aiken's 4th Northern Division was an exception for reasons that are complex and not relevant to this study.

than to bring about a republican Dail as he had always professed and as he had striven with de Valera to achieve.

All these things considered therefore Collins' intentions seem clear and purposeful, and they were to achieve a ceasefire and then convene the republican Dail he had worked so hard to create. The fatal shot put an end to that.

The evidence – circumstantial though it may be - that Collins, having seen his modest solution to the Four Courts situation develop into nationwide civil war, intended to resolve matters quickly and bring about the Sinn Fein coalition parliament, is persuasive.

As part of his stated intention to "try to end this thing", Collins, chairman of the IRB, had arranged a meeting of IRB officers, neutral and from both sides, for Desmond's Hotel in Cork.

Col. Frank Thornton was directed by Collins to arrange the meeting. Thornton contacted and spoke to Liam Deasy, who passed him on to Liam Lynch and Tom Hales. Thornton was ambushed and wounded en route. Nonetheless and confirmed to me by IRB-men Florrie O'Donoghue, Liam Deasy and Sean O Muirthile, arrangements for the meeting proceeded.

Emmet Dalton has been cited in support of the view that no meeting was intended. Dalton was not a member of the IRB and for that reason - as he confirmed to me - would not have known about it.

The IRB had always been Collins's essential power-base. But that would-be decisive meeting of IRB officers in Cork - neutral and from both sides with that end in view - on Tuesday, August 22nd, the day he was killed fell, like the leader himself, into a glowering and despondent dusk over the infertile fields and ditches of Beal na mBlath.

It is inconceivable to imagine Collins contemplating with anything but horror a civil war such as continued. Not alone because of the appalling incidents and events, but also because of how it would have affected his carefully calculated plans and purpose concerning the entire country.

This is not a version of the so-called "Stepping-Stone" argument, though some comparison is unavoidable. It is to outline from an assessment of the facts such as we know them the most probable scenario at that time.

The civil war was fought initially between troops of the Provisional Government, backed by that government and the disputed second Dail, the general Establishment and - eventually – by the Irish Free State army (from December 6th, 1922) and by a majority of the population backed up by British power and influence, against the Volunteer Army Executive and its troops on its own.

From the time of the outbreak of hostilities on the 28th June 1922 to his death Collins was the single most powerful figure in the country. Although, when he assumed the duties of commander-in-chief he had, nominally, stepped down as Chairman of the Provisional Government, he continued to exercise control over and to instruct that cabinet[92](W. T. Cosgrave was acting chairman while Collins was on active service). Besides controlling the Army of the Provisional Government, Collins was chairman of the IRB; he remained a committed republican; he was in more sympathy with those on the other side than with his own supporters.

John Redmond's old Irish Party membership, wiped from the political blackboard of Ireland in 1918, together with the general commercial, religious and professional establishments, rolled in to strengthen the pro-Treaty side, with the result that Collins, the republican, found himself in the ironic position of drawing most of his support from those for whom he had little but contempt and being most strongly opposed by those with whom he had most in common. More than any other single event the death of Collins became pivotal, hardening pro-Treaty attitudes and coinciding with the irresponsible decision of the Executive forces to continue a guerrilla campaign when

---

[92] Mr. Liam Cosgrave, former Taoiseach, confirmed to the author that this was so in the following reply to the question: "I have always understood that my father's position at that time was that of acting Chairman".

they were already beaten in the field and had lost the support of a majority of the populace.

After Collins's death matters deteriorated badly particularly in Kerry, where atrocities by pro-Treaty troops became the subject of a government enquiry. "Matters" as de Valera expressed it, "fell into the hands of lesser men."

Neither Sinn Fein, the only party in Dail Eireann, nor de Valera (except briefly at the beginning as a junior officer), played any role of significance regarding the conduct of the war. De Valera, who had neither power nor authority over the anti-Treaty forces, nonetheless, like Collins, tried to bring hostilities to an end and did his utmost to end it and have the Coalition Dail agreed by Collins and himself convened.

From the start the Army Executive, suddenly unexpectedly thrown into civil war, made several major errors of judgement. The Republic which they supported was threatened with either peaceful constitutional restructuring or, as they then perceived it, with armed attack. To the former they were prepared to give a chance until the détente with their colleagues in the Four Courts and the attack on it a few hours later threw them willy-nilly into the field of Mars. Yet in taking the field they supported no significant alternative political opposition and, while their opponents prepared pragmatically for the foreseeable, took no practical steps either to avoid possible civil war or conduct one effectively if that became unavoidable. De Valera and some of his anti-Treaty Sinn Fein colleagues – including the tragic and symbolic figure of Cathal Brugha – were exceptions and worked from the outset to halt the escalating war, calling for a cease-fire as early as July.

With the outbreak of hostilities the anti-Treaty forces had two positive military options. First an overwhelming assault by road and rail on Dublin from the south and west to take over government; secondly guerrilla warfare. (A third possibility might have been a concerted attack on the North with the hope that it would win the support of the pro-Treatyites, as proposed by Tom Barry). In the event they formed a static line from Limerick to Waterford - the so-called 'Munster Republic' - and waited to be attacked; probably the weakest military option short of surrender open to them.

There were at that stage four governments in the country. These were Dail Eireann; the Provisional Government, and the Northern and Southern Governments formed under the 1920 Act, (the last never functioned and was essentially subsumed by the Provisional Government).

The War resolved nothing that could not have been resolved without it. It created an enduring bitterness that lasted until the Emergency of World War Two and stultified political progress and development for years. It certainly affected the outcome of the Boundary Commission which might otherwise have endorsed a four-county Northern Ireland, as proposed by Churchill and Lloyd George.

As to what might have happened had Collins not been killed and the fateful meeting at Desmond's Hotel had taken place that night, this is best summarised in his own words to his brother Sean before leaving Sean's house to set out for Cork on that Tuesday: "I'm going back to settle this thing."[93]

---

[93] See *Life and Death of Michael Collins*, p. 112.

APPENDICES

APPENDIX 1
Plans allegedly submitted to Germany

Spindler *(pp 246/247)* refers to and outlines the 'Irish Revolutionary Directory' plans (from America) to the German General Staff, as follows:

A. In Ireland, Beginning of February 1916.

I. *On England's Side:*
a) British troops, roughly .... 30,000 strong
poorly trained, few competent officers, no trained non-commissioned officers, little artillery and few machine-guns, all of old pattern.
Location: 3-4 training camps for recruits, remainder in small garrisons, In Dublin 3,000, in Limerick 1,000 soldiers (all recruits).
b) Irish Police................10,000 strong
efficient, all armed with rifles [read carbines], distributed in quite small detachments throughout country.
Total   40,000 strong.

II. *On the Side of the Revolutionary Directory:*
a) *Assured*: Irish Volunteers .....40,000 strong
Trained as efficient as the American National Guard; having 10,000 rifles various pattern, mostly Lee-Enfields with 200 rounds apiece. (They can further obtain possession of a further 20,000 rifles of inferior quality but practically without ammunition). There is a lack of superior officers.
b) *Anticipated:* Redmond Volunteers 50,000 strong

scattered, not well trained. It is reckoned that practically all of them will join the revolution.

c) *Probable*: Many thousands of unorganised Irishmen, provided they can be armed.

B. Support in the form of persons and arms *from America* is impossible.

C. *Proposition:*
Support from Germany:

25,000 to 50,000 rifles with cartridges, proportionate number of machine-guns and field artillery as well as a few superior (sic!) officers to be sent on transport ship to Limerick taking northern route and escorted by submarines. (Even for 100,000 rifles the necessary number of men would be obtainable).

It is obvious - bearing in mind, for instance, the 1,500 guns landed at Howth - that Irish resources were, for whatever reason, considerably over-stated, perhaps to indicate to the Germans that the proposition was more viable than it was.

Proclamation of the Republic, 1916

POBLACHT NA h-EIREANN
The Provisional Government
of the
Irish Republic
To the People of Ireland

IRISHMEN AND IRISHWOMEN: In the name of God and of the dead generations from which she received her old tradition of manhood, Ireland, through us, summons her children to her flag and strikes for her freedom.

Having organized and trained her manhood through her secret revolutionary organization, the Irish Republican Brotherhood, and through her open military organisations, the Irish Volunteers and the Irish Citizen Army, having patiently perfected her discipline, having resolutely waited for the right moment to reveal itself, she now seizes that moment and, supported by her exiled children in America and by gallant allies in Europe, but relying first on her own strength, she strikes in full confidence of victory.

We declare the right of the people of Ireland to the ownership of Ireland and to the unfettered control of Irish destinies, to be sovereign and indefeasible. The long usurpation has not extinguished the right, nor can it ever be extinguished except by the destruction of the Irish people. In every generation of the Irish people they have asserted their right to national freedom and sovereignty; six times during the past three hundred years they have asserted it in arms. Standing on that fundamental right and again asserting it in arms in the face of the world, we hereby proclaim the Irish Republic as a Sovereign Independent State, and we pledge our lives and the lives of our comrades-in-arms to the cause of its freedom, of its welfare and of its exaltation among nations.

The Irish Republic is entitled to, and. hereby claims, the allegiance of every Irishman and Irishwoman. The Republic guarantees religious and civil liberty, equal rights and equal opportunities to all citizens and declares its resolve to pursue the happiness and prosperity of the whole nation equally and oblivious of the differences carefully fostered by an alien government, which have divided a minority from the majority in the past.

Until our arms have brought the opportune moment for the establishment of a permanent National Government, representative of the whole people of Ireland, and elected by the suffrages of all her men and women, the Provisional Government hereby constituted, will administer the civil and military affairs of the Republic, in trust for her people. We place the cause of the Irish Republic under the protection of the Most High God, Whose blessings we invoke upon our arms, and we pray that no one who serves that cause will dishonour it by cowardice, inhumanity or rapine. In this supreme hour the Irish nation must, by its valour and discipline and by the readiness of her children to sacrifice themselves for the common good, prove itself worthy of the august destiny to which it is called.

Signed on behalf of the Provisional Government
Thomas J. Clarke, Sean MacDiarmada, P. H. Pearse, James Connolly, Thomas Mac Donagh, Eamonn Ceannt, Joseph Plunkett.

APPENDIX 3

Beal na mBlath –
How was Collins killed?

On August 22nd, 1922, Michael Collins was killed in action during the Civil War at Beal na mBlath, West Cork, not far from his birthplace.

That tragic event has been the subject of controversy ever since – much of it silly and acrimonious and often based on such dogmas as: – "I've studied it, therefore I'm right", when citing little more than second-hand answers (years after the event); these remain selective hearsay, not fact.

The tendency to force facts to fit a theory, and superficially plausible inferences like: - "'X' said that 'A' said he shot a soldier. 'A' was a decent man who wouldn't lie." "I remember exactly what he said 50 years ago." "He was a marksman, therefore couldn't miss." "It was a dum-dum bullet, therefore the wound was big at the back." "There was a small entry wound in Collins's forehead, so it wasn't a ricochet", have added to the confusion.

An unpublished, but reliable, survey of the ambush site was made in the late 1940s by Lt. Gen. M. J. Costelloe and Tom Barry. Their conclusions were similar to my own, which they called "definitive"[94].

In the absence of conclusive evidence we must rely on inference, nevertheless the circumstantial evidence provides a reasonably clear and precise picture.

---

[94] The author's books *The Civil War in Ireland* (1966) and *The Life and Death of Michael Collins* (1968), contain, respectively, the first published collated account of the ambush from participants on both sides and the first published detailed comparative analysis of it. No published commentaries add to this, and some have been misleading. These two accounts probably form the basis for most subsequent ones.

These are essential facts:-

1. One of the six ambushers fired a single rifle-shot at a specific target at about the time that Collins was hit;
2. Collins was struck and killed as the result of a large wound behind his right ear;
3. It was dusk and the light was poor.

The main points of dispute centre on
A. Who fired the fatal shot?
B. Was it direct or indirect (i.e. ricochet)?
C. Was there also a frontal wound?
D. The bullet - normal, coated high-velocity .303, 7mm Mauser or 'dum-dum'?
E. Where was Collins when he was hit? Was he standing, or not? In what direction was he facing? And, last, but not least,
F. Where did he intend to go that evening?

Some of these questions are readily answered.

Virtually beyond doubt the fatal shot was fired by Denis 'Sonny' Neill of Kilbrittain, one of the six-man anti-Treaty clearing party that fired on the convoy to warn their dispersing comrades of its approach from behind. He'd been a British army territorial and was considered a good shot – not a 'marksman'.

The action is reported to have lasted 30 to 40 minutes, a surprisingly long time for such a minor fire fight.

The six 'ambushers' came under considerable fire from the Vickers machinegun in the armoured car, from the convoy troops armed with Lee Enfield rifles and, allegedly, Thompson (Tommy) sub-machine guns and at least one Lewis light machinegun. "There was little chance to raise our heads let alone get an aimed shot off in dusk at all", said one of the ambushers, Jim Kearney.

After about twenty minutes the Vickers gun developed a stoppage. John McPeake, the gunner, deafened from the noise of the machine-gun in the confined space of the armoured-car turret and nauseous from cordite fumes, raised the (then) circular hatch cover to clear it. (The hatch and cover were later changed).

During this "lull" Neill fired his aimed shot at an approximate range of 150-190 yards. It was the only shot fired by any of the ambushers at that point.

His verbal report to Liam Deasy, Divisional 2i/c stated: "I saw a head coming out of the armoured car and I fired at it."

The contemporary statement of McPeake states: "As I raised the hatch cover 'whang!' a bullet hit it and blew off a lug."

Given the poor light, being under fire, the subsequent realisation that Collins had been killed (and time lapse), the most probable picture that emerges is that Collins was killed either by the ricocheting bullet or by the lug. Factor in that Collins evidently stood in the lee, right (south) of the armoured car and it goes a long way to resolving the difficulty presented by the (large) wound being behind the right ear, otherwise out of the line of enemy fire, but not of a ricochet off the armoured car.

Dr. Oliver St. John Gogarty, who performed the autopsy on Collins in Dublin's College of Surgeons, had experience treating wounded soldiers during WWI. He had no love for the anti-Treaty side. Nevertheless he was adamant that the (single) wound was caused by a ricochet.

While remaining conjectural this outline ties up most of the loose ends and accommodates to the facts without recourse to notional forehead entry wounds unperceived by Gogarty, etc.

It also renders the notion of a 'dum-dum' bullet irrelevant.

The dum-dum was a flat-nosed, half-coated lead rifle bullet, not unlike a revolver bullet, originating in the Indian town of that name. It expanded on striking, causing a large, ugly wound. Of limited range, it was notoriously erratic. The standard coated .303 rifle bullet can be readily modified - i.e. by abrasion - to approximate a dum-dum, with similar effect, and often was during WWI. It is known to have been used in Ireland by the Black and Tans and Auxiliaries.

While there is still some question about it on the balance of probabilities "Sonny" Neill is the most likely one to have fired the fatal shot. Neill, although he acknowledges having aimed at a live target, could have had no idea who that target was. Secondly it is virtually beyond question that Neill's round was the one that struck the armoured car and "blew off" the lug and, thirdly, as noted above that it was either the lug or the ricocheting round that took Collins behind the right ear.

The facts are clear. Neill was there. He fired at least one shot (probably more) at 'the enemy'. It would be absurd to think that his intention was other than to do so with effect. There were very few other shots fired from his side. Collins was killed in the action.

Both Deasy and Jim Kelliher quote him that he fired at a human target near the armoured car at about the right time. Tom Barry, M. J. Costelloe and Florrie O'Donoghue were also of the opinion that the fatal shot was fired by him – allowing for the fact that the evidence is inconclusive.

The number of men on the hill who fired at all was small. Given that the fatal shot *was* fired by one of them, candidates are very few and "Sonny Neil" is by far the strongest. All shots fired by anyone in the action (on either side) were fired in wartime at the enemy.

Given also that he fired at least one shot about the time the Vickers gun stopped mowing the hedgerows/and Collins was killed, and given that the total number of shots fired by the republicans was very small, it is hardly feasible to eliminate him as a likely source. To rule out the possibility that he may have fired the fatal shot would be absurd.

Following the shooting there was considerable intensity of feeling and emotion in the locality, especially in the Provisional Government Forces. In particular there was concerted focus of blame on John McPeake, the gunner in the armoured car, to the extent that, in fear for his life, he sought and was given help from the republicans to desert the Provisional Government forces and get back to his native Scotland.

When I was writing the Civil War *(The Civil War In Ireland)* during the 1950's and '60's it was widely believed that he was responsible for shooting Collins. After publication of my book the focus shifted and Emmet Dalton became the 'assassin' – a sleeper mysteriously planted by the British who, in his wisdom, waited his opportunity (without having the slightest idea that it would present itself) and then, over a distance of some 50-80 yards and across other members of his unit, while under fire, shot Collins dead with a Webley revolver. This nonsense achieved powerful currency – even to the extent of being the central thesis of a book.

In the 1950's I spoke to many of those on both sides about the ambush, including Liam Deasy, Mick Galvin, Tom Crofts, Florrie O'Donoghue, Jim Hurley, Tom Kelliher, Dan 'Sando' Donovan, Pete Kearney, Emmet Dalton, Tom Barry, M. J. Costelloe.

The long and the short of it is that Collins was killed in this action. He was killed either a/ accidentally or b/ deliberately by i/ one of the enemy or ii/ one of his own side. There are no other possibilities.

It seems unlikely - barring a complete fluke – *that any shot other than Neill's* from the republican side could have been the fatal one.

Certainly Deasy and the retiring group fired some token rounds from their elevated position (as may have some of a Kerry group making their way home who had nothing to do with the Beal na mBlath meeting). The likelihood of one of these being the fatal bullet is remote.

That leaves the possibility that the shot came from his own side – *vide* the absurd and wrong rumours about Dalton and McPeake.

The real tragedy of Beal na mBlath is that Collins, the only fatal victim, was also the only man who possessed the all-round power to end the conflict, which he had committed himself to doing at the IRB meeting on that point that evening, and bring the prorogued Coalition Dail into being in September as agreed.

Short Bibliography: Some Further Reading

Akenson, D. H. and Fallin, J. F., *The Irish Civil War and the Drafting of the Free State Consitution*, (Eire-Ireland), September,1970.

Andrews, C. S., *Dublin Made Me*, Cork 1979.

Beaslai, Piaras, *Michael Collins and the Making of a New Ireland*, (2 vols.),Dublin, 1926.

Birrell, Augustine *Things Past Redress*, London, 1937.

Boyd, Andrew *Holy War in Belfast*, 1970

Butt, Isaac *The Famine in the Land*, London 1847.

Caulfield Max *The Easter Rebellion*, London, 1964.

Charteris, John *Diaries of,* Dublin.

Churchill, *Life of Lord Randolph Churchill*.

-    *Aftermath*, London, 1929.

Collins, Michael, *Arguments for the Treaty*, (ed.)   Dublin, 1922.

Colum, Padraic, *Arthur Griffith*, 1959.

Connolly O'Brien, Nora, *Portrait of a Rebel Father*, Dublin 1955.

Coogan, T. P. *Michael Collins*, London 1990.

Curtiz, Liz, *The Cause of Ireland*, Belfast, 1994.

Dangerfield, George, *The Strange Death of Liberal England*, New York, 1935.

Deasy, Liam *Towards Ireland Free*, Cork, 1973.

Devoy, John, *Recollections of an Irish Rebel*, Shannon, 1969.

Duffy, Gavan, *The League of North and South*, 1886.

Duggan, John P., *A History of the Irish Army,* Dublin,1991.

Dwyer, T. Ryle, *Michael Collins and the Treaty; His differences with deValera,*   Cork, 1981.

Fox, R. M., *James Connolly*, Tralee, 1946.

Goblet, Yann Morvran, *L'Irlande dans le Crise Universelle, 1914-1920*, Paris 1920.

Greaves, C. Desmond, *1916 as History; the Myth of the Blood Sacrifice*, Dublin, 1991.

Hart, Peter (ed.), *British Intelligence in Ireland, 1920-21*, Cork, 2002.

Healy, T. M., *The Great Fraud of Ulster*, Dublin, 1917.

Horgan, J. J. *The Complete Grammar of Anarchy*, London, 1918.

Keogh, Dermot, *Twentieth Century Ireland; Nation and State*, Dublin, 1994.

Lawlor, Sheila, *Britain and Ireland*, 1914-23, Dublin 1983.

Lee, J. J., *Ireland 1912-1985; Politics and Society*, Cambridge, 1989.

Longford Earl of and O'Neill,T.P, Eamon de Valera, 1970.

Lowe, C.J. and Dockrill, M.L., *British Foreign Policy, 1914-1922* (2 vols), London 1972.

Lloyd George, David, *Is It Peace?,* London 1923.

Macardle, Dorothy, *The Irish Republic*, Dublin, 1951 (new edn.)

McEoin, Sean, *1919 to the Truce* (article in *With The IRA in the Fight for Irish Freedom*, Tralee, (no date).

Mackey, Herbert O. *The Life and Times of Roger Casement*, Dublin, 1954.

Macready, General Sir Nevil, *Annals of an Active Life*, London, 1924.

Martin F. X.(ed.), *Leaders and Men of the Easter Rising*, Dublin, 1967.

McGarry, Fearghal (ed.), *Republicanism in Modern Ireland*, Dublin, 2003.

Montieth, Robert, *Casement's Last Adventure*, Dublin 1953.

Murphy, Brian, P., *Patrick Pearse and the Lost Republican Ideal*, Dublin, 1991.

Neeson, Eoin, *The Civil War*, Cork, 1966;   Dublin, 1997.

    -   *The Life and Death of Michael Collins*, Cork, 1968.

    -   *Birth of a Republic*, Dublin, 1998.

Nowlan, Kevin B., *The Making of 1916*, Dublin, 1969.

Noyes, Alfred, *The Accusing Ghost*, London, 1957.

O Broin, Leon, *Dublin Castle and the 1916 Rising*, Dublin.

O'Connor, Frank, *The Big Fellow*.

O'Donoghue, Florence, *No Other Law* Cork, 1963.

O'Hegarty, P. S., *History of Ireland Under The Union, 1801-1922*, London,1952.

O'Neill, Brian, *Easter Week*, Dublin, 1936.

Pakenham, Frank, *Peace By Ordeal*, London.

Pearse, P. H. *Manifesto,* Collected Works.

Ryan, Desmond, *The Rising*, Dublin, 1949.

    (ed.) - *The Study of a Success*, P. H. Pearse, Dublin, 1917.

Spindler, Karl, *The Mystery of the Casement Ship*, Berlin, 1931.

Talbot, Hayden, *Michael Collins' Own Story*, London, 1923.

Taylor, Rex, *Michael Collins*, London, 1985.

210

Townshend, Charles, *The British Campaign in Ireland 1919-1921*, London, 1975.

Whyte, John H., *1916 – Revolution and Religion; the Easter Rising*, (ed. Martin).

Williams, T. Desmond, *Eoin MacNeill and the Irish Volunteers*, (ed. Martin).

Wilmore and Pimlott, *Strategy and Tactics of War*, London

MAP 1

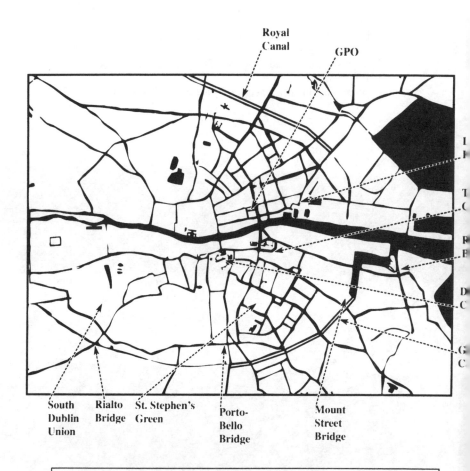

Royal Canal

GPO

I
F

T
C

R
F

D
C

G
C

South
Dublin
Union

Rialto
Bridge

St. Stephen's
Green

Porto-
Bello
Bridge

Mount
Street
Bridge

The map shows some of the places occupied or intended to be occupied by the
Volunteers together with other important features of Dublin, such as the canals,
between which most of the action in 1916 occured.

MAP 2

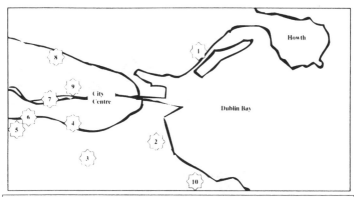

The British held some ten major barracks or positions around Dublin City stretching from Dollymount to Mount Merrion. They were as follows:-
1, Musketry School, Dollymount. 2, Beggars' Bush Barracks. 3, Portobello (Cathal Brugha) Barracks. 4, Wellington (Griffith) Barracks. 5, Richmond Barracks. 6, The Royal Hospital. 7, (Clancy) Barracks. 8, Marlborough (McKee) Barracks. 9, Royal (Collins) Barracks. 10, Bombing School at Merrion. In addition were smaller garrisons in Dublin Castle and Ship Street Barracks.

MAP 3

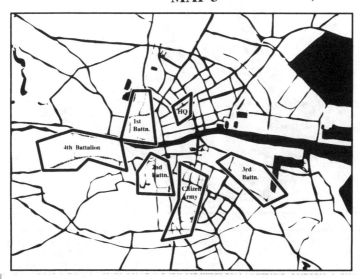

The map shows some of the places occupied or intended to be occupied by the Volunteers together with other important features of Dublin, such as the canals, between which most of the action in 1916 occured.

213

MAP 4

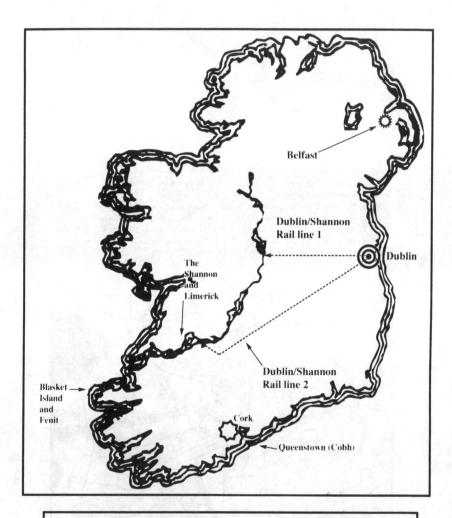

Belfast

Dublin/Shannon
Rail line 1

Dublin

The
Shannon
and
Limerick

Dublin/Shannon
Rail line 2

Blasket
Island
and
Fenit

Cork

Queenstown (Cobh)

The map shows the areas involved in the plan and general action of 1916, including the rail routes south and west intended to be taken by the Dublin Volunteers to link up with the Volunteers from Cork, Kerry and Limerick and the locations of Aud in the Blasket sound and where she was sunk outside Cork Harbour.

MAP 5

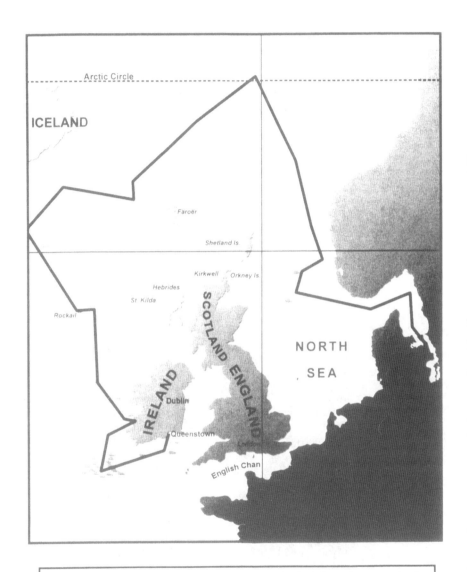

The Map shows the route taken by the arms ship Aud from Germany to the Blasket Sound in 1916 and to where she was scuttled outside Cork Harbour.

INDEX

218

Publications from the Aubane Historical Society

∞ A North Cork Anthology, *by Jack.Lane* and *Brendan Clifford*
∞ Spotlights On Irish History, *by Brendan Clifford*
∞ The 'Cork Free Press' *by Brendan Clifford*
∞ Piarais Feiritéir: Dánta/Poems, *with translations by Pat Muldowney*
∞ Elizabeth Bowen: "Notes On Eire". Her espionage reports to Winston Churchill
∞ Kilmichael: the false surrender. A discussion
∞ Thomas Davis, *by Charles Gavan Duffy*
∞ Extracts from 'The Nation', 1842-44
∞ Na h-Aislingí - vision poems of Eoghan Ruadh O'Súilleabháin *translated by Pat Muldowney*
∞ Aubane versus Oxford: a response to Professor Roy Foster and Bernard O'Donoghue
∞ The burning of Cork; an eyewitness account *by Alan J Ellis*
∞ With Michael Collins in the fight for Irish Independence *by Batt O'Connor T.D*
∞ Michael Collins: some documents in his own hand. *Introduced by Brian P. Murphy*
∞ Sean Moylan in his own words: His memoir of the Irish War of Independence
∞ An Answer to Revisionists *Eamon O Cuiv and others*
∞ A Narrative History of Ireland/Stair Sheanchas Éireann by *Mícheál Ó Siochfhradha*
∞ James Connolly Re-Assessed: the Irish and European Dimension *by Manus O'Riordan*
∞ Six days of the Irish Republic (1916) and other items *by L. G. Redmond-Howard*
∞ Envoi - taking leave of Roy Foster by *Brendan Clifford, David Alvey, Julianne Herlihy, Brian P Murphy*
∞ The Origins and Organisation of British Propaganda in Ireland 1920 *by Brian P Murphy OSB*
∞ Was 1916 A Crime: A debate from Village magazine
∞ The Pearson Executions in Co. Offaly *by Pat Muldowney*
∞ Seán O'Hegarty, O/C 1st Cork Brigade IRA *by Kevin Girvin*
∞ Fianna Fail and the decline of the Free State *by B. Clifford*
∞ The Shakespeare Conspiracies: untangling a 400 web of myth and deceit *by Brian McClinton*

Orders to: jacklaneaubane@hotmail.com

221

ON OTHER BOOKS BY EOIN NEESON:

The Civil War in Ireland: "Astonishingly objective and impartial" – *Ernest Blythe*, the Irish Times.
"Eoin Neeson ... has done the State much service...'
Gabriel Fallon, Catholic Herald.

A History of Irish Forestry: "... a fascinating story, rooted in scholarship and splendidly told. Eoin Neeson's fine book will be the standard text for years to come ..."
Laurence Roach, Irish Independent.
"*This important study is to be applauded...*" *Con Costello*, Leinster Leader.

Birth of a Republic: "...a passionate and stimulating read ... obviously the culmination of decades of thought and research..."*Con Costello*
" This incisive and compelling narrative is by far the best book on the period I have read", *Dick Roche*, Irish Independent
"Eoin Neeson lays before us the reality and then asks – and answers – the essential questions. As always this book is enlivened by both the questing detachment of the historian and the lively, memorable prose of the author." *Maire Brugha*